INDO-JUDAIC STUDIES
Some Papers

To
my brothers
DAVID W. DAVID
and
the late SHIMON DAVID
and
my friend from school and Oxford days
ADITYA KUMAR BHATTACHARJI

INDO-JUDAIC STUDIES
Some Papers

Yohanan ben David
(*formerly* Samson John David)

NORTHERN BOOK CENTRE
New Delhi

Icons on Cover

Shri Chakra. The Mandala is held to be a potent centre of psychic energy, a consecrated enclosed space separated from the profane by barricades of magical figures and by 'guardians' at the doors. The central point is called the bindu, 'drop', and represents the focal area of psychic power.

Shield of David. The lower symbol is the Shield of David as it appeared in King Solomon's Temple at Jerusalem.

Cover Concept & Design: Akanksha Singh & Prasad

ISBN 81-7211-131-2

Price: Rs. 150.00, £ 10.00, $ 12.00

Published by Northern Book Centre, 4221/1, Ansari Road, New Delhi-110002; Phones: 3264519, 3271626; 3280295; Fax: 011-3252651; E-mail: nbcnd@ndb.vsnl.net.in and printed by Paragon, New Delhi

Introduction

Work on Indo-Judaic Studies is pioneering as the researcher finds himself on virgin territory. The subject has not yet been recognised as an academic discipline but if the present trend continues it could be accepted as a mainstream course at universities in the not too distant future. There is a vast mine of information yet to be explored.

The reasons why Indo-Judaic Studies was hardly known until quite recently are manifold. First, India and Israel did not have full diplomatic relations for over four decades. Second, the Indian historians seemed to have been unaware of the Jews in India or tended to mix them up with Muslims, Zorastrians (Parsees) and Christians. Third, the Jews in India formed just 0.01% of the total Indian population so they kind of got lost in a vast mass of humanity. Finally, Jewish history has been dominated by western Jewish historians who have paid more attention to European history than to the histories of the oriental Jewish communities. Jews in India (if they knew that such a community existed) were usually mentioned in a chapter that could have had the title, "Remote Communities and Lost Tribes"!

During the last ten to fifteen years oriental Jews in Israel and elsewhere have been storming the bastians of western Jewish dominance. They have also realised that their histories need to be rescued from outsiders. Having said this, it does not mean that no work had been done in Indo-Judaic Studies before full diplomatic relations were established. There have been anthropologists mainly and a few historians who have addressed the subject. They were, however, very few and far between.

Not any more. The field of Indo-Judaic Studies is now being occupied not only by anthropologists and historians but also by demographers, sociologists, political scientists, linguists, art historians and experts in comparative religion. This volume is basically an historical study though there is one section on Art.

5th April, 2002   *Yohanan ben David*

Acknowledgements

I wish to thank the following for their financial assistance:

the Cecil Roth Trust of England; the World Sephardi Organisation of Israel; the Israel Free Loan Association; the Israeli banks: Discount, Mizrachi, Leumi, First International, Ḥapoalim; the British Bank, Barclays; the Jacob Sassoon Trust of Mumbai; and the Indian Council of Historical Research at Delhi.

The following also deserve mention:

Hariyadi and Endang Wirawan; Dr. (Mrs.) Sangh Mittra; Dr. Beni and Mrs. Dalia Padai; Hananiah and Irit Ezra; the Ben-Zvi Institute Library at Jerusalem; Akanksha Singh and Yosef De Carvalho Fonseca..

5th April, 2002   *Yohanan ben David*

Contents

GANDHI
AND THE
ZIONISTS

(including C.F. Andrews and the Jews)

Gandhi, the Jews and Zionists; using Olsvanger's 1936 India Diary as a Case Study

Gandhi wrote that he was surrounded by Jews in South Africa. The best known of these was Henry Polak. It was Polak who gave Gandhi Ruskin's book, *Unto This Last*. This book inspired Gandhi to set up the Phoenix Settlement in Durban. However, Gandhi's closest friend, indeed, his "soul friend", was Hermann Kallenbach. Sarojini Naidu told Dr. Immanuel Olsvanger, the Zionist emissary to India, that "Polak is not like Kallenbach; he (Polak) makes money out of India"[1]. Mahadev Desai, in a long article on Kallenbach in *Harijan*, started by recording that Kallenbach was a giver. He ended with a quote from Kallenbach: "I was a German; I am now Jew".[2]

Kallenbach was a successful architect. He was a bachelor; reserved and introspective. He kept his private papers hidden away in an attic in his house in Johannesburg.[3] He had living in his house his niece, Hannah Lazar, and her daughter, Isa.[4] It was they who found his papers after his death in 1945 and brought them to Israel.[5]

What Emerges from the Papers?

Kallenbach saw the greatness in Gandhi when the latter was still an ordinary lawyer in South Africa. Gandhi's Jewish secretary,

---

1. Entry in Olsvanger's 1936 India Diary at the Central Zionist Archives in Jerusalem. Olsvanger's papers are at the CZA and the Genizim (the archive of the Association of Hebrew Writers in Tel Aviv). Special thanks to Olsvanger's grand daughter, Ms Ruth Ramon Almagor, for assistance over a period of three years.
2. *Harijan*, June 5, 1937, Vol. V, No. 17. The quotation in full: "Mr Kallenbach is a princely giver, and believes in earning in order to give". See also *Harijan*, May 29, 1937, Vol. V, No. 16.
3. It is believed that he requested Gandhi to destroy his personal letters as he did not want these read by a third party. It is not clear whether Gandhi actually did so.
4. This is the Isele of the Gandhi correspondence. She is now Dr. Isa Sarid. The author of this paper wishes to thank her for granting him access to the Kallenbach papers.
5. They also buried his ashes at Kibbutz Degania.

Sonia Schlesin, was introduced to Gandhi by Kallenbach. Gandhi stayed for some time in Kallenbach's home in Johannesburg. Doke, who wrote the first biography of Gandhi, wrote the book in Kallenbach's house. However, he does not mention Kallenbach once in his book. It was Kallenbach who asked for an English version of *Hind Swaraj*. Gandhi complied by dictating it in English while Kallenbach took it down. Kallenbach took an active part in the "Satyagraha" movement and even went to jail with Gandhi. He it was who bought Tolstoy Farm near Johannesburg. When Gokhale visited South Africa in 1912, he stayed with Kallenbach. There are two original letters written by Gokhale in the papers. Gokhale thanks Kallenbach for his hospitality and adds how can India ever thank him for what he has done. It was Gokhale who advised Gandhi to bring Kallenbach along with him to India. Kallenbach's luggage actually gets to India but not Kallenbach himself: he was detained in England as an enemy alien (he was then a German subject) and spent the First World War in a camp on the Isle of Man. The papers also record Kallenbach's falling out with his family over his support for Gandhi. One of his brothers asks him to see a psychiatrist. Kallenbach agrees and then writes back saying that he is no eccentric.[6]

The papers also put C.F. Andrews in a new light. There are over forty letters of Andrews to Kallenbach. These letters show Andrews' sympathy for the Jews; the work he did finding asylum in India for Jewish refugees fleeing the Holocaust; and his active support of Zionism. After reading his letters to Kallenbach and going through his papers at Vishva-Bharati in Santiniketan, I am convinced that "CF" was a "gentile Zionist".[7]

The Jewish sages have written that if one wants to know whether one is truly welcome in a house one should watch the behaviour of the children and the dog. If, for example, the children receive one well then one can be sure that one is truly welcome. One of the most touching things of the Kallenbach papers are the letters that Gandhi's children wrote to him. There

---

6. In a letter dated March 10, 1913, to Ms. Mayo, a friend in Scotland, Kallenbach wrote that as a Jew he felt it his duty to support the Indian minority in South Africa.

7. A non-Jew who supported the Jewish aspiration for a homeland in Palestine. This group included Lord Balfour, David Lloyd-George, and Winston Churchill. Here it should be pointed out that not all Jews were Zionists.

are two files of these. One son, Manilal, who remained in South Africa, was treated like a son by Kallenbach. The Jewish sages have also said that a man should listen to his wife when it comes to inviting guests to his home. Gandhi's wife, Kasturba, was fond of Kallenbach and she was very upset when Kallenbach was put in a detention camp and could not accompany Gandhi to India.

Having said this, the Jews that Gandhi knew were less religious and more humanist.[8] However, Gandhi did learn something of Judaism from them. In an interview Gandhi gave to the *Jewish Chronicle* of London in 1931, he said that he attended services two or three times at a synagogue in Johannesburg. He also said he kept Passover with his Jewish friends going to their homes every night.[9] He heartily enjoyed eating the unleavened bread as he thought it "very nice and crisp". He then added: "I cannot say I have made a proper study of the Jewish religion but I have studied as much as a layman can".[10] However Gandhi read the so-called Old Testament[11] in translations made by Christians. So it is not surprising that one finds him making the following statement in an issue of *Harijan* dated 17.12.1938:

> Indeed it is a stigma against them (Jews) that their ancestors crucified Jesus. Are they not supposed to believe in an eye for an eye and tooth for a tooth.

He used the Christian translation "chosen race" for the Hebrew word "amsagolah". The Jewish translation is "treasured people", that is, a people who must strive for higher virtue. Then he crowned it all by saying that the Jews were the "untouchables of Christianity". Despite these unsavoury interpretations and translations, there is no evidence of malice towards the Jews on the part of Gandhi. He just had not realised the Christian agenda.[12] The best proof that Gandhi held no malice towards the Jews lies in the Kallenbach papers. When Kallenbach visited Gandhi in 1937 and again in 1939, he offered to bequeath all his

8. See Margaret Chatterjee: *Gandhi and his Jewish Friends* (London, 1992).
9. Passover lasts eight days outside Israel.
10. Jewish Chronicle, October 2, 1931.
11. The Jews call it the Tanak.
12. ˙ Pandit Nehru too records that he took part in Jew-baiting while he was at Harrow school in England as he thought it was an English social custom!

wealth to Gandhi. He could trust Gandhi to put it to good use maybe to build hospitals for the poor. However Gandhi told Kallenbach to give the money to help his suffering people. When Kallenbach died in 1945, a South African Jewish newspaper wrote the following:

> Hermann Kallenbach, a famous architect in South Africa, bequeathed his entire fortune of 80,000 (pounds sterling) to funds in Eretz-Israel (Palestine) .... It was Gandhi who advised Kallenbach to leave his money to Eretz-Israel, thereby giving his support to the aspirations of the Jewish people.[13]

There is no need in this paper to dwell on the reasons why Gandhi supported the *Khilafat* movement and why he later agreed not to raise Palestine at the Round Table Conference. When I met Narayan Desai, the son of Mahadev Desai, early in 2000, he allowed me to read a pre-publication copy of his new book entitled *My Gandhi*. In it Desai makes a very important point about Gandhi. He writes that Gandhi said that when he made a number of statements on a topic, the last one had to be accepted as his final opinion on the matter. Gandhi made a final statement on Zionism in July, 1937. This he gave to Kallenbach who handed it over to the Jewish Agency's Political Department. The statement is now in the Central Zionist Archives in Jerusalem. For some reason it is not included in the Gandhi-Kallenbach correspondence in the National Archives at New Delhi. Before looking at the statement it is necessary to trace the events that led up to it.[14]

Why did the Zionists Target Gandhi in the 1930s?

First, Gandhi, like Einstein, was an international figure. Einstein had already been won over to Zionism. Second, the Zionists were concerned at the activities of the Mufti of Jerusalem. He had

---

13. Translation from the Yiddish newspaper *Die Zeit*, Johannesburg, South Africa, May 7, 1945.
14. P.R. Kumaraswamy: Mahatma Gandhi and the Jewish National Home: An Assessment (University of Haifa journal, "Asian & African Studies", Vol. 26, 1992); and Gideon Shimoni: Gandhi, Satyagraha and the Jews; A Formative Factor in India's Policy towards Israel (The Leonard Davis Institute for International Relations, Hebrew University of Jerusalem, 1977).

visited India to raise funds for the renovation of the Holy Places in Jerusalem. From the Nizam of Hyderabad alone he had received 17,000 pounds sterling.[15] Third, the Zionists felt that he was using the Ali brothers, Mohammad and Shaukat, to magnify the Palestine problem into an Islamic one. The correspondence of Chaim Weizmann, Israel's first President, attests to the alarm in Zionist circles when the Mufti offered to bury Muhammad Ali in Jerusalem. Finally, there was a perception among the Zionists that British policy in Palestine was determined by Muslim public opinion in India.

The Head of the Jewish Agency, the political arm of the Zionist movement, was Moshe Shertock—better known as Moshe Sharett, Israel's second Prime Minister. Sharett, in his political diary, expressed excitement when he heard that Gandhi had a "yedid nefesh" (soul friend) who was Jewish. He wrote immediately to Kallenbach. The letter is a long one, very well written, and can be considered a Zionist policy statement. Its main points were that since the Jews were returning to Asia, they needed support from countries on that continent; India could provide marketing and economic advantages; the Hindu politicians saw Jews as Westerners intruding on Palestine so it was necessary to placate them and get a favourable response from them; and it was important to act immediately before opinions hardened. Sharett wanted Kallenbach to go out and use his connection with "the greatest of living Hindus" for promoting the Zionist cause. Kallenbach agreed to help. The idea was that he would accompany Dr. Immanuel Olsvanger to India. However, business commitments prevented him from going out at the appointed time but he urged Olsvanger to go on ahead. He would follow later.

Dr. Immanuel Olsvanger was a Sanskrit scholar who translated the Gita into Hebrew.[16] His aim, as he himself put it, was to "learn, teach, and to spread knowledge of the great Indian culture among Hebrew readers and thus build another layer in the spiritual bridge between Mount Sinai and Mount Meru". He had been abroad several times on lecture tours raising money for

---

15. .He raised in India 22,000 pounds sterling in all. See Sir Martin Gilbert: *Jerusalem in the Twentieth Century* (Chatto & Windus, 1996) p. 107.
16. 1888–1961. He wrote his diary in German. For details of his life see entry "Olswanger" in the *Encyclopaedia of Zionism and Israel*.

the Zionist cause. During one of these trips he met Mrs Sarojini
Naidu in South Africa. As this was his first trip to India (he
visited there four time more), Naidu took him under her wing, as
it were, and introduced him to all the leading figures in the
Indian nationalist movement. Olsvanger wrote: "From the first
moment on she treated me as her friend and felt obliged to show
me all hospitality possible".

Olsvanger arrived in India on August 12, 1936, and left on
November 7, 1936. The first entry in his diary is dated August 19
and the final one October 29. Through Naidu's good offices he
met Pandit Nehru as early as August 20. This is how he
described that meeting:

> First visit with Sarojini at Jawaharlal. Mixture of
> nationalism, which he admits, socialism, even
> communism, but not fully agreeing with Sovietism. A
> slim, beautiful man, but not very clever. He is very
> proud of knowing "the affairs of the world" with all
> their implications. All implications, that is, British
> Imperialism. Lives with his sister who is married to a
> strict vegetarian Jain. Rich house, just as he is very
> rich. Clothes typically Indian; he personally in
> Congress clothes. He doesn't know anything about
> Zionism; has seen Palestine once as he flew over the
> country. Maintains, though, to know Zionism and its
> connections with "the affairs of the world".

From this first meeting one begins to suspect that something
was going wrong. There was no meeting of minds. Olsvanger, by
the way, is probably the only man to describe Nehru as "not so
clever"!

Immediately after this meeting with Nehru, Olsvanger
wrote:

> Sarojini told me I should ask Laemmel for an
> interview by writing a letter to his secretary Mahadev
> Desai in Wardha and should mention my
> acquaintance with Kallenbach.

Throughout his diary, Olsvanger could not get himself to call Gandhi by his real name. Instead he used "Laemmel"—a Yiddish word which translates as "little lamb". However, it becomes obvious as the diary goes on that Olsvanger meant the word in its derogatory sense, that is, "simpleton".[17]

Olsvanger had another two meetings with Nehru and there was also an exchange of correspondence. What emerged was that as Nehru was against imperialism, he wanted the British out of Palestine. He felt that the Zionists and the Arabs should settle their differences by negotiating directly. He suspected that the Zionists were seeking the support of the British. He wrote to Olsvanger wishing that "the Jews did not rely so much on the British government and would make a settlement directly with the Arabs". He had a point. While Olsvanger was in India, Sharett, his boss, set up the "Notrim" (Guardsmen). This Jewish Supernumerary Police was recruited by the British for defence duties during the Arab Revolt (1936–39). Olsvanger admitted in his diary that "this could become difficult for me with regard to Jawaharlal".

Olsvanger's meeting with Gandhi, that should have been the high point of his trip to India, turned out an anti-climax:

A very weak Laemmel sat on his bed just recovered from his illness. On the floor sat about fifteen of his students. I got a place at the edge of the bed. I talked with him for about twenty minutes. I disliked the whole environment. But nobody could notice it. I told the rebbe everyting in detail. The rebbe was silent and the students listened. He told me that Kallenbach had telegraphed and told him he would be with him by the end of October. He was looking very much forward to that letter. When I told him that Kallenbach was a very active member of the South African Zionist Federation, he said: "I know. But then he has so many poor relatives"! That's how he understands Zionism! I decided to let Kallenbach deal with this goat-hero. When I realised he was really very weak, I said goodbye. He struggled to get up but couldn't manage. He said very heartily goodbye and

---

17. The sense in which it is being used could also mean "tramp".

asked me to visit him once again if I was still in India
when Kallenbach arrives.

Politically Olsvanger's mission turned out a failure. The
word "politically" should be emphasised as there were other
areas where Olsvanger's visit was a success. He met
Rabindranath Tagore and the poet agreed to send his works to
the Hebrew University in Jerusalem. He raised money for the
Zionist cause. Perhaps his greatest achievement was finding
Hayeem Samuel Kehimkar's history of the Bene Israel Jews in
India. This had been lying around in manuscript form since 1897.
Olsvanger took it and had it published in Tel Aviv in 1937. The
publication of this book played a big part in drawing the
attention of world Jewry to the Bene Israel. The Bene Israel have
since been eternally grateful to Olsvanger.

After his failure to win Gandhi's support for Zionism,
Olsvanger grew bitter and this bitterness finds expression in his
diary. For example, he started to repeat rumours about Gandhi
as though they were fact. He related that Gandhi asked for some
monkeys to be killed. He hinted at some kind of romance
between Gandhi and, as he put it, "the half-mad Annie Besant".
He went on to say that Gandhi's influence was on the decline
and that he was no longer the undisputed leader of the Indian
people.[18]

Kallenbach visited Gandhi after Olsvanger's trip. His first
visit was in 1937 and his second in 1939. In a letter from India to
Sharett, Kallenbach hinted at why Olsvanger failed in his mission
to win the support of Gandhi for Zionism:

> .... I felt—and still feel—the 23 years of separation
> non-existent. Just as in South Africa we eat together
> and sleep next to each other. It is a different world to
> the West, with which the great part of our people and

---

18. Abraham Shohet, an Indian Jew of Iraqi origin, the Zionist representative in
    India and editor of "The Jewish Advocate" in Mumbai, gave a much more
    accurate report. He reported back that "Gandhi is India". In conversations
    with me in Israel in 1998 (recorded on tapes by his daughter, Aviva Ben Hefer
    of Haifa), Shohet confirmed that he had disagreed with Olsvanger's
    assessment of the importance of Gandhi. There is a letter from Gandhi to
    Shohet in the Manuscript Department of the National Library in Jerusalem.
    Shohet is mentioned in Olsvanger's diary.

we, I feel sorry to say, have so fully associated themselves. Perhaps this is one of the reasons, why we have not been able so far to overcome some of our difficulties in Palestine, with its eastern habits and culture.

There is here, and what I have been able to observe elsewhere, much simplicity, the people are natural and so humanised that one cannot but wholeheartedly associate himself with them. I feel at home here .....

There are great and urgent problems in front of M.G. and his band of unselfish and untiring workers, concerning the fate of many millions of people. Notwithstanding this M.G. has an open heart and a ready ear for all comers who pour their troubles, hopes and joys into this receptive and so understanding soul and so he also listens patiently to me.......[19]

In July, 1937, Gandhi made his final statement on Zionism and gave it to Kallenbach. It stated:

Assuming that Zionism is not a material movement but represents the spiritual aspirations of the Jews, the introduction of Jews in Palestine under the protection of the British or other arms is wholly inconsistent with spirituality.

Neither the mandate nor the Balfour declaration can therefore be used in support of sustaining Jewish immigration into Palestine in the teeth of Arab opposition.

In my opinion the Jews should disclaim any intention of realising their aspiration under the protection of arms and should rely wholly on the goodwill of Arabs.

No exception can possibly be taken to the natural desire of the Jews to found a home in Palestine. But they must wait for its fulfilment till Arab opinion is

---

19. The letter has the dateline "c/o Mahatma Gandhi, Tithal, Bulsar", and is dated June 1, 1937 (Kallenbach papers).

ripe for it. And the best way to elicit that opinion is to rely wholly upon the moral justice of the desire and therefore the moral sense of the Arabs and the Islamic world.

What about the Jews who have already settled in Palestine? Under the moral or ethical conception they would be governed by the same considerations as are applicable to the newcomers. But I have little doubt that immediately the support of physical force is disclaimed and the Jewish colony begin to depend on the goodwill of the Arab population their position would be safe. But this is at best a surmise. My opinion is based purely on ethical considerations and is independent of results. I have no shadow of doubt that the existing position is untenable.[20]

Needless to say, the Zionists were disappointed by this statement. C.F. Andrews too was unsatisfied. His letter to Kallenbach probably summed up the general feeling in Zionist circles:

> ...... I am *not* (sic) satisfied with Bapu's own statement. It seemed to me too abstract ...... I may do more to make clear the true Jewish position with which I have such deep sympathy here in India and this may be better than going at once to Palestine ..... I am unsatisfied with his present position. I regard it as an imperfect one, not an untrue one ....[21]

Olsvanger's bitterness spilled over into the Zionist movement. Like Olsvanger they too tried to discredit Gandhi. They succeeded to a certain extent to hold Gandhi up to ridicule over the advice he gave the Jews in Nazi Germany. He told them to resist Hitler non-violently and even be prepared to commit mass

---

20. CZA S253587.
21. Dated August 11, 1937; dateline "c/o Seth Jamnalal Bajaj, Wardha" (Kallenbach papers). C.F. Andrews was working on a book on the life of Christ and had intentions of visiting Palestine. However, he neither made it to Palestine nor did he complete the book. Kallenbach had even given "C.F." money to help pay for the trip. When Andrews died in 1940, Kallenbach requested that the sum be given to Andrews' relatives.

suicide. There was at least one attempt to trip him up. The Zionists approached Gandhi and told him that by his opposition to the consumption of alcohol he would make it difficult for Jews to practise their religion.[22] Gandhi was naturally upset as he respected all religions. He immediately wrote to Kallenbach in South Africa and the latter turned to the Chief Rabbi at Johannesburg for an authoritative opinion. The Chief Rabbi ruled that "the wine need not be fermented". The attempt by the Zionists to tar Gandhi with the anti-semitic brush failed in this instance.[23]

In conclusion, Gandhi could well have the last word. In an issue of *Harijan* in 1938, he wrote:

> Let the Jews who claim to be the chosen race prove their title by choosing the way of non-violence for vindicating their position on earth. They can add to their many contributions the surpassing contribution of non-violent action.

At least one prominent Israeli did not disregard Gandhi. This was David Ben-Gurion, Israel's first Prime Minister. He had just one picture in his house at Kibbutz Sde Boker in the Negev desert. This was a picture of Mahatma Gandhi.[24]

---

22. On Sabbaths (Friday evenings and Saturdays) and Festivals, Jews recite special blessings over wine.
23. See "The Jewish Tribune", October 1939, p. 15. col. 1, for a full report. This journal was published in Mumbai and was edited by the late David I. Sargon and his brothers. Sargon's mother was Iraqi and his father Cochini. An obituary on Sargon appeared in the "Journal of Indo-Judaic Studies", Vol. 1, No. 2, April 1999.
24. The author of this paper has researched Ben-Gurion, the spiritual man. See his book, "These Days Will Never Come Back" (Northern Book Centre, New Delhi, 2002) p. 39.

Author's Introduction to the Olsvanger 1936 India Diary

Dr. Immanuel Olsvanger (1888–1961)[1] visited India five times and, as he put it, was "proud and happy to treasure the friendship acquired with many". This Diary is a day to day record of the visit he made in 1936 as a Zionist emissary.

His papers in the Central Zionist Archives in Jerusalem and the "Genizim" (the archive at the Association of Hebrew Writers in Tel Aviv) contain no account of his other visits.[2] They consist mainly of letters to and replies from prominent Indians and Israelis. His correspondence with Pandit Nehru has been included with this Diary (Appendix 1).

This visit of Olsvanger was important for the Zionists. They had already won the support of Albert Einstein to their cause; they were now eager to win over the other outstanding international figure—Mahatma Gandhi. There was also an important local consideration: the Mufti of Jerusalem, Hajj Amin al-Husayni, had targeted the some 70 million Muslims living in India in an attempt "to magnify the Palestine Problem into an Islamic one".[3]

The original intention was that Olsvanger would be accompanied by Hermann Kallenbach, one of Gandhi's Jewish friends from South African days (see exchange of letters between Shertok (Sharett) and Kallenbach included with this Diary, Appendix 2). It was pity that the latter could not make it at the appointed time as they would have made a formidable duo. Olsvanger knew Sanskrit [4] and had already travelled widely as a

---

1. For details of his life, see entry "Olsvanger" in the *Encyclopaedia of Zionism and Israel.*
2. His family too have no records. Special thanks to his grand daughter, Ms. Ruth Ramon Almagor, for assistance over a period of three years.
3. See page 4 and footnote 15 in article by P.R. Kumaraswamy, "Mahatma Gandhi and the Jewish National Home: An Assessment", in University of Haifa journal, "Asian and African Studies", Vol. 26, 1992.
4. About his translation of the Bhagvad Gita into Hebrew he wrote: "My aim was to learn, to teach and to spread knowledge of the great ancient Indian culture among Hebrew readers and thus build another layer in the spiritual bridge between Mount Sinai and Mount Meru".
   See also his correspondence with Nehru (Appendix 1).

lecturer for Karen HaYesod (Zionist Foundation Fund) Kallenbach's rapport with Gandhi would have made up for Olsvanger's lack of sympathy for the Indian leader. With the benefit of hindsight, Kallenbach's urging Olsvanger to go to India ahead of him turned out to be a mistake. Politically Olsvanger's mission was not a success and he himself remarked in his Diary: "I decided to let Kallenbach deal with this goat-hero".[5]

Perhaps the greatest result of this journey was in the field of scholarship—the receipt of Hayeem Samuel Kehimkar's manuscript on the history of the Bene Israel.[6] Yet there is not one word about this in the Diary even though there are references to meetings with the Bene Israel. This is a glaring omission.[7] Though the Diary ends abruptly (in mid sentence), there is no reason to believe that an entry referring to Kehimkar's history is missing. Olsvanger arrived in India on August 12, 1936, and the first entry in his Diary is dated August 19; he left on November 7, and the final entry is dated October 29. Could he have thought that the piece he wrote in the book which he arranged to have published in Tel Aviv in 1937 was acknowledgement enough?[8]

Olsvanger took a genuine interest in the Bene Israel right upto the time of his death and they have never forgotten him as a result. The following tribute is an example of their affection for him:

> How gracefully he had moved about with the Bene-Israel, both rich and poor, in the cities and in the villages, seeing for himself our way of life. He took it

---

5. Kallenbach did go to India in 1937 and 1939 and was more successful in his dealings with Gandhi than was Olsvanger, though, in the end, the Zionists were disappointed with Gandhi's response.
6. However Olsvanger did collect 3600 Rupees (in cash and pledges) in Calcutta and about 2500 Rupees in Bombay (*The Jewish Tribune*, December 1936; p. 6, col. 3). His visit again to India in 1941 was to raise funds for Keren HaYesod in order to make up for the loss of 300,000 pounds sterling a year in contributions from countries that had been taken over by the Nazis (*The Jewish Tribune*, April 1941, p. 11, col. 2).
7. Thanks to Mr. Artur Isenberg for pointing this out when he read the Diary in the original German. He it was who advised that it would be worth translating in full.
8. What Olsvanger did with the original manuscript is not clear. It appears he returned it to the Kehimkar family. The late Mrs. Shirley Berry Isenberg traced it to a family member in Canada but he refused to let her see it.

upon himself to publish the History of the Bene-Israel of India, written by the late Mr. Haeem Samuel Kehimkar, founder of the Bene-Israelite School in Bombay. Dr. Emmanuel Olswanger was a honest historian; as such he did not twist facts. Thus he has done a great service to our community and has earned its everlasting gratitude.[9]

The existence of the Diary is not new.[10] However this is the first time it has been published in its entirety in English. It speaks for itself. The translator has tried to keep the author's telegraphic style in translation.

---

9. Shofar (journal of the Federation of Indian Jews), Issue No. 3, May 1972 (Jerusalem). Olsvanger said, "The question is often asked whether the Bene Israel are of pure Jewish race. The only reply that I can make is that they are as pure a Jewish race as the European Jews are" (The Jewish Tribune, April 1937, p. 10, col. 2; and The Jewish Advocate, April 1937, p. 10, col. 2.)

10. See Joan G. Roland: *Jews in British India: Identity in a Colonial Era* (published for the Brandeis Univ. Press by the Univ. Press of New England, 1989); and Gideon Shimoni: "Gandhi, Satyagraha and the Jews; A Formative Factor in India's Policy towards Israel" (The Leonard Davis Institute for International Relations, Hebrew University of Jerusalem, 1977).

The Diary at the Central Zionist Archives, Jerusalem

Translated from the German by Ms. Edelgaard David,
former teacher at the International People's College,
Elsinore, Denmark

19.8. Today visited at Meyer Nissim,[1] a rich Bagdad merchant, who wants to be seen as a European. He knows everything about Palestine, has all the sympathies but doesn't want to be involved with it officially, and I should't ask him to be President at my meeting even though he promises to be there—"out of respect". He is afraid that a closer cooperation between the Jews in India could lead to them being declared non-Europeans.[2]

19.8. Sarojini[3] phoned just now, at 8 p.m., that I should see her tomorrow to go together to Jawaharlal[4]. She is charming in every respect. I went a day early with Shohet[5] to her brother Chattopadhyaya from whom I learnt that Sarojini stays at the Taj[6]. I sent her some lines and reminded her of our meeting in Johannesburg and London and of Mrs. Kuper and Kallenbach.[7]

1. Head of the Bombay (Mumbai) Municipal Corporation and later Mayor of Bombay.
2. For the Baghdadi Jews' efforts to be classified as Europeans, see Roland: *op. cit.*, pp. 57, 58, and 59–61.
3. Naidu, the poetess, who had already shown deep sympathy for the Jews (see enclosed report of her 1916 address to the Bene Israel and Olsvanger's letter to her. Appendix 3)
4. Pandit Nehru.
5. Head of the Zionist and Keren HaYesod office in Mumbai and editor of *The Jewish Advocate*. He was born in Iraq in 1913 and lived in India from 1926 to 1953. He then settled in Israel.
   His daughter, Aviva ben Hefer of Haifa, recorded on tapes conversations he had in 1998 with the author.
   There is a letter from Gandhi to Shohet in the Manuscript Department of the National Library in Jerusalem.
6. The luxury hotel in Mumbai, not the Taj Mahal.
7. He died in 1945 in Johannesburg and his cremated remains were buried at Kibbutz Degania in Israel. His collection of over 5000 books he left to the

(Contd.)

She remembers every detail even the little disagreement that she evoked at one of her lectures in Johannesburg. From the first moment on she treated me as her friend and felt obliged to show me all the hospitality possible. When I told her what it was all about, she thought it as something self-evident: "Well, of course, I don't see why the Jews should not colonise Palestine".

20.8. First visit with Sarojini at Jawaharlal's. A mixture of nationalism, which he admits, socialism, even communism, but not fully agreeing with Sovietism. A slim, beautiful man, but not very clever. He is very proud of knowing "the affairs of the world" with all their implications. Implications, that is, British imperialism. "Silneje koschki zwierya nyet"[8]. Lives with his sister who is married to a strictly vegetarian Jain. Rich house, just as he is very rich.

Clothes typically Indian; he personally in Congress clothes. He doesn't know anything about Zionism; has seen Palestine once as he flew over the country. Maintains, though, to know Zionism and its connection with the "affairs of the world" very well. The discussion couldn't last long since he had to go to a meeting with the All India Congress Committee. I should visit him though in a few days and have dinner with him. Sarojini told me I should ask Laemmel[9] for an interview by writing a letter to his secretary Mahadev Desai in Wardha and should mention my acquaintance with Kallenbach and Laemmel's son.

21.8. Interview with the editor of the *Times of India* who immediately sent me his chief reporter. That boor scribbled some lines down and that was the interview. The editor himself has no opinions and will surely write articles that contradict each other: sometimes juicy; sometimes milky; sometimes parve.[10]

The visit at Parrera, the editor of the *Evening News*, was very different. A Christian from Goa; extremely intelligent; knows the problem of Zionism very well; knows Iraq but not Palestine. His

---

Hebrew University (thanks to Dr. Joel, Mrs. Marcus, and Mr. Goldberg of the National Library at Jerusalem for assistance in locating the books. Thanks also to Dr. Isa Sarid for access to her grand uncle's papers). See Margaret Chatterjee: *Gandhi and his Jewish Friends* (London, 1992).

8. There is no animal stronger than a cat.
9. The reference is to Gandhi and is a Yiddish term meaning "young lamb" or, in this context, a "simpleton" or even "tramp".
10. Neither meat nor milk—fish, for example.

sympathies are absolutely on the side of Zionism which he often expresses in his paper.

22.8. Sarojini just stops in front of my hotel to take me to a meeting of the Congress that's been led by Jawaharlal. With her is a Mr. Vielsinger from America who lives in Shanghai. A big tent, decorated with red, white, green flags with spinning wheel in the white strip. Benches, chairs, desks, for the guests and delegates. The platform covered with long, white cushions on which the gentlemen and ladies of the presidium are sitting among others Jawaharlal and Sarojini. Everywhere a humming of big fans and in front of the speaker there is placed a microphone. After Jawaharlal's speech, there are two more Indians speaking and then an ailing leader of the Socialists who gets a chair. The assembly is opened by a *Kol Nidre*-type[11] song that's sung by a tall Indian with black, curly hair who also plays on a Tambura (a harp—a long neck with a gourd-like belly and four strings). The Tambura sounds like the crying of a reasonably musical cat. Then Jawaharlal is reading resolutions of condolence for those who have passed away. After each one, we stand up. Every now and then a smile on the faces of the men with white Gandhi caps. Sarojini is mercurial. During the whole procedure she introduces me to different delegates, whispers something into their ears that evokes interest and respect for me. I also meet Miss Bharati Sarabhai whom I had met on the boat. She was beautiful in her sari. She greeted me in Indian fashion and introduced me to her brother and cousin who all urged me to come to Ahmedabad where their father is one of the richest millowners in India and an influential member of Congress.

At Sarojini's request I was driven home in an official Congress car.

24.8. In the afternoon, visit to Congress. Debate about languages. Resolution to introduce Hindustani by force as the only language in Congress voted down by a small majority. Splendid English speaker Satyamurti from Madras who doesn't understand any Hindustani. I should talk to him in Madras.

---

11. Name of the prayer that is chanted on the evening of the Fast of Yom Kippur (Day of Atonement).

24.8. After an hour, Mrs. Loeffler is supposed to accompany me to an Indian dance. I am quite excited.

In the *Evening News* of today the "chamer"[12] of a reporter tells that I have come as a representative of the "Palestine Delegation Fund".

Agreement at Congress, after being introduced to Devh, the ailing Socialist, to visit him in Benares.

Talked also with Bulabhai Desai, the well-known lawyer. He was pleased about the greetings from Eliasch and Assaf and asked me to greet them back. "Sarojini spoke to me a lot about you. I shall be glad to see you in a few days".

24.8. In the evening, after the Congress, Shohet and I visited Harindranath Chattopadhya (called Harin), for the second time. He lives with his sister who is a teacher in Lahore. He is a wellknown poet, knows "Habima"[13] when it was in Russia and then in Berlin.

24.8. In the evening, dinner at Hutheesing's, Jawaharlal's brother-in-law. This time he gives the impression that he is genuinely interested in Palestine and asks for literature and some addresses in P. I gave him the addresses of Herrmanns (Leo) and "Davar". Sarojini promises to introduce me to Abdulghaffar Khan[14]. She takes me from Hutheesing's house to the Congress building where there is a reception in honour of A., the "Frontier Gandhi", as he is called. Sarojini places me on the dais which I leave immediately. Sarojini starts her speech in English because of me but she is strongly required to continue in Hindustani. There was no chance to talk to Abdul during the evening; still Sarojini promises to arrange for an interview with him. This evening she takes me to a special performance of an Indian film, specially performed for the Congress. At the same time she orders lawyer, Dr. Munshi, a prominent Congressman, to invite me to an Indian meal; and Brelvi,[15] the Muslim editor of the *Bombay Chronicle* to give me an interview. At the reception Abdul got presented with many garlands, among others, from a

---

12. Hebrew (donkey). In this context, "stupid".
13. Jewish theatre that has now found a permanent home in Tel Aviv.
14. The Pathan leader who accepted Gandhi's philosophy of non-violence.
15. S.A. Brelvi was a bitter critic of the Zionist Movement.

socialist association, a Christian association, and the Bombay Stock Exchange.

A dialogue in the house of Hutheesing:

Sarojini: There are many beggars, widows, and prostitutes in India.

Jawahar: Why you should name widows and prostitutes in one breath, I fail to understand.

Sarojini: Well, one leads to the other, poor things!

In the evening at six, I drove with Sarojini to an assembly of the newly founded Civil Liberties Union. When Jawarhalal saw me from the dais, he greated me Indian style with special friendliness which made everybody look at me. A beautifully disciplined crowd that filled the hall of the Theosophical society to the limit. I walked behind Sarojini making sure I got through the crowd. All speeches witty and elegant in English. Enormous respect for Jawahar and Sarojini. Each of her sentences is greeted either with hearty laughter or thunderous applause.

Opponents of Congress also participated in the meeting. One of their representatives, an adopted son of Sarojini, a Muslim, said that the newly founded Union had to fight the advancing Congress if they tried to suppress civil liberty just as they were fighting against the suppression of civil liberty now.

Jawahar nodded in agreement.

25.8.   Last night at 10.30, to the cinema with Sarojini. Earlier on when she didn't know yet whether she would be able to come, she wrote a chit saying I should be placed next to Jawaharlal. She works incessantly for the Congress in spite of her weak heart and she really looked exhausted. In the cinema she introduced me to the Mayor of Bombay and some other dignified Muslims whose names I couldn't remember. They asked for details on Palestine and our work there and mocked the idea that it should hold a danger for Islam. The unrest in P. was the same as the periodically appearing unrest between Muslims and Hindus in India. I couldn't talk much to Jawaharlal this time since he had to leave the cinema early. The film dealt with Indian village life and the disastrous impact of the money lenders there. I got the impression by Jawahar's behaviour (later he also confirmed it to me) that he doesn't like village life.[16] There are about 200,000 villages in India. Of course Jawahar needs the sympathy of the Muslims here at the moment as the country is preparing for new elections to the Legislative Assembly. The whole assembly isn't more than a vegetarian beefsteak but the mouth is still watering to get a bite at it. He will surely try to please the Muslims in order to get their votes.

His first step against Zionism because of anti-imperialistic motives has brought him a welcoming letter from Toller.[17] And since he knows that Toller is Jewish, for him this was an encouragement.

I told Jawahar later of the car accident and what one of the Indians had told me. He answered: "Quite possible, but this is a terrible tragedy".

26.8. Today I expected an answer to my letter to Jawahar. Didn't come.

26.8. I visited the BI[18] doctor, Dr. Abraham Erulkar, Imperial House, Lamington Road. He used to take great interest in the Congress but had to give it up because of overwork as a doctor. He was for a while the personal doctor of Laemmel. He is an Indian nationalist, a grandson of Divekar.[19] He talks about the contradiction between Zionism and Indian nationalism just as we know it from other countries in the world. He asked me whether he or other BI's would be accepted as equals by the Jews in Palestine. When I strongly confirmed that they would, he lifted up his sleeve and asked with surprise: "What, with this skin"? I put my hand alongside his and he laughed. He complained

16. It was perceptive of Olsvanger to notice this as this turned out to be one of the major points of disagreement between Nehru and Gandhi. The former believed in modernising India through industrialisation; the latter wanted to develop the villages and return Indians to the simple life.

17. The German playwright and revolutionary who converted from ultranationalism to pacifistic socialism. If Toller was involved in the car accident that Olsvanger mentions immediately after, he was not killed as he committed suicide three years later apparently out of a feeling of despair when Franco's Fascists defeated the Republicans in Spain. Toller had sided with democracy. See entry in *Encyclopaedia Judaica* for more details of his life.

18. Bene Israel Jews who are believed to have lived in the Reigad area of India from at least 175 B.C.E.

19. He built in Mumbai in 1796 the Bene Israel's first synagogue—"The Gate of Mercy".

about the attitude of the Jews in South Africa towards the Indians to which I answered mentioning Kallenbach (who he knew) and the other Laemmel Yidlach.[20] I reported in detail about everything that's being done in P.; about the kinds of agricultural settlements; about the revival of the Hebrew language; and he was—I got the impression—shaken. The grandson of Divekar got lively again. Among other things, I told him: "Doctor, I don't think one should attach so much importance to one's personal views that are influenced by casual personal experiences and interests, when it concerns a movement that lived and struggled for realisation under a hundred different economical and political structures and constellations". These words made him serious. He promised to come to my meeting with the BI and asked me at any rate to visit him once again. He is, by the way, married to a British Christian. Moshe's talk in the Assifat Hanivcharim on August 18, '36, could become difficult for me with regard to Jawahar. Others will welcome it.[21]

26.8. Eight hours in the evening. Just back from a visit at Sarojini's. I proposed to her to come to the opening of the Indian department at the Hebrew University of Jerusalem. She answered that she couldn't venture such a tour at the moment, among other things, because of the severe illness of her daughter who is just recovering from an operation. She might be willing to come in March 1937. She asked me also not to be annoyed about my failing to interview Abdul because I would meet him at Laemmel's (he cannot stand the climate of his usual place at this time of the year).

---

20. Yiddish for "little Jew" (used in a derogatory sense). He is referring to Gandhi's other Jewish friend, also from South African days, Henry S.L. Polak.

21. There is no entry for August 18 in Moshe Sharett: *Making of Policy: The Diaries of Moshe Sharett*, edited by A. Malkin, Tel Aviv, 1968. However, judging by the entries for August 15 and August 22 and the situation in Palestine, the reference is to Sharett's idea of setting up the "Notrim" (Guardsmen). This Jewish Supernumerary Police was recruited by the British for defence duties during the Arab riots (Revolt) of 1936 to 1939. These started with an Arab general strike lasting from April to October 1936 organised by an Arab High Command led by the Mufti. Olsvanger had been sent to India by Sharett, then Head of the Political Department of the Jewish Agency, so one can understand his difficulty as Nehru had made it clear that he was against imperialism and that he wished the "Jews did not rely so much on the British government and would make a settlement directly with the Arabs".

27.8.   Sarojini phoned at 10.30 this morning that I should come across immediately. I arrived there limping with a bit of fever and pains in my legs. Some of the Socialists of the Congress were assembled there. It was agreed to hold a 'Conversatione' about P. in 3–4 days.

She repeated that she would like to come to Jerusalem in March but she couldn't say anything right now. I should come to tea at 5 o'clock.

At three I met the Congress Parsee Nariman who recommends me to Heerji Nahidin, the editor of the Parsee newspaper *Kaiser Hind* with regard to literature for the library. He (Nariman) will come to the 'Conversatione'.

At 5, at Sarojini's, who is a very charming hostess. She has taken all the trouble to make real coffee for me accompanied with a selection of Indian sweetmeats. I met her third adopted son who, like the others, is a Muslim. That's why she is so popular with many Muslims. This adopted son is a nephew of the lawyer Jinnah[22] who stands outside Congress. He listened with interest to what I had to say about P.; expressed his sympathy; and thought that we shouldn't get excited about the attitude of certain Muslim circles because they didn't express the mood of the Indian Muslims who are not at all interested in P.

My legs scream with pain; I would prefer to go to bed. But in 2 hours I have to go to the assembly of the BI.

28.8.   The assembly with the BI is very well attended. The presidium was headed by Mr. Aptekar and Mr. Solomon Moses, solicitor. What I told them about P. they listened to with open ears. Some wanted to know whether they could start a colony of BIs in P. I said it was definitely possible if they showed enough interest. I believe we would gain a lot if we had a big number of BIs in P. Besides the purely Jewish point of view, Judaism would also get richer as one shouldn't underestimate what the spirituality of India would bring to P. One would also create a living contact with India and the fact that many of them (the BIs) have an equally good contact with Hindus as with Muslims could be beneficial to us. In the discussion some wanted to know whether there was a danger of an outnumbering of the Arabs by the Jews and whether this was justified.

---

22.   Later founder of Pakistan.

31.8. Dinner, according to Sarojini's recommendation, with the Parsee R.P. Masani, N.M. Wadia Charities, 120 Bazaar Street, Bombay, Grand Hotel.

Also there was his son, one of the leaders of the Socialist Congress Party. Father for Zionism; son against because anti-imperialist. The son's opinion I changed a little. The father would like to found here Kibbutzim with younger Parsis because he hopes that the idealistic way of life would keep the young people with the Parsi faith. He asks for detailed literature about history, development and government of the Kibbutzim. Also his son asks me to send material to the Congress House in Bombay. The father promises to get me books for the library.

The article in the *Evening News* was very friendly. The *Bombay Chronicle* gave my interview a prominent place. Afterwards the journalist Brelvi wrote an anti-Zionist article.

3.9. Since 31.8, I'm in bed. Nevertheless I went to the assembly of the KH,[23] that was led by the lawyer Judah Meyer Nissim, who first didn't want to know anything about the assembly, but then asked at the last moment to have his name printed on the visitor's list anyway. However, he didn't come to the assembly; I think because he was afraid that he had to sign something and because he got to know that Sarojini would be present.

My lecture and the answering of the questions evoked enthusiasm, especially with Sarojini who didn't stop congratulating me.

Yesterday, assembly of the Socialists—the 'Conversatione'. Sarojini introduced me and Y.J. Meherally presided. The chairman, a strict opponent of Zionism, closed with remarks that I had made "quite a good case" for Zionism; they (the Socialists) ought to get more information; and on the whole my answers were diplomatic.

When a person from the assembly asked me whether the British policies in P. were similar to the one in India, and I was about to answer, Sarojini shouted: "What does he know about the policy in India, he is hardly a month here". I was very grateful for that.

Laemmel, in the meantime, got seriously ill. My visit postponed. Maybe I will see him in a few weeks' time.

---

23. Karen HaYesod.

Sir Vijayaraghavacharya is talking Tuesday, 8.9, on "The Mandates: Syria, Iraq, Palestine".

8.9. In hotel "Green" an assembly of the "progressive group" under the chairmanship of an Englishman, an editor from *The Times of India*. Sir Vijaya was speaking. He reported realistically and objectively about Palestine and his facts were exact. He also tried to be objective in judging the problem—Jews and Arabs. Nevertheless, the lecture was, on the whole, in our favour. The auditorium consisted for the greater part of Indians—Hindus and a few Muslims—and many Englishmen. A few Jews were present. Mr. Fuchsman, a Swiss Jew, left the hall as soon as Sir V. started to talk about Palestine. I sat at a table together with Sarojini, Shohet and Leser. After the lecture, Sarojini asked me whether I wanted to speak. I replied that I didn't think that my entering the debate was necessary. She answered, "but I think so", and she got up immediately and said: "Mr. Chairman, we have here in our midst Dr. O. who comes from P. and I think you should invite him to place before us the Jewish point of view". Thus she forced me to get up on to the stage and to speak. My words—I spoke for about 20 minutes—were greatly applauded, even by some Muslims, especially when I emphasised the wish of the Jews to live with the Arabs and Islam in traditional friendship. A Muslim expressed the thanks of the assembly on behalf of the Chairman with a faint touch of pro-Muslim opposition to Zionism. My words as well as the lecture of Sir Vijaya resulted in an overall impression in our favour.

10.9. Maulana Irfan, General Secretary of the Khilafat Committee, Khilafat House, Love Lane, Bombay (Tel: 41706). I got to know him accidentally while visiting an Indian music school that was run by a Muslim together with Sarojini. He took my address, visited me, and asked for me to visit him. I did so and found him in company of his secretary and publisher of an Urdu newspaper in Bombay. That one told me that he had read my interview in the *Bombay Chronicle* and understood from that interview that it is the principle of the Jews in P. that the Arabs shouldn't earn a pice—and that's what he reported in his paper. In my interview I had said that we followed the principle in our agricultural colonies not to employ any foreign worker. I explained everything to the publisher in detail. He said: "Well, that is a different matter altogether! I quite appreciate that, and I will correct my statement in one of the next issues". Whether he has done it or not I do not know as none of our people reads Urdu or bothers to follow the Indian newspapers (Urdu, Hindi, Bengali, Gujarati, Marathi).

Both the publisher and Irfan thought the best solution would be an opening of Transjordan for Jewish immigration and he (Irfan) would be prepared to defend his view at the Palestine Conference that's taking place in the middle of October in Delhi. Besides, he invited me to participate in that conference and either to speak in the forum or "to have a friendly talk" with individual delegates. Written to Mosche about Hantke today. The Zionists here are of the opinion I should't do it because Irfan and his company are a dangerous crowd; they would twist my words whatever I'd say and use it for their own purposes.

Sarojini thinks I should accept the invitation.

13.9. I tried in vain to meet Desai and Jinnah. Desai was in a hurry to go to Simla. Jinnah excused himself a thousand times and said he had to leave the same evening "and besides I'm not interested in the Palestinian question. I would love to meet O. nevertheless. I heard so much about him from Sarojini". I met the solicitor K.M. Munshi, 111 Esplanade Road, Fort Bombay. Goes in completely for Zionism. The Muslims were the same everywhere and he wouldn't give a dime for their words either in Palestine or in India. England had all the reasons to support our cause. Further, a meeting with H.S.L. Polak, Imperial Indian Citizenship Association, Sohrab House, 235 Hornbey Road, Fort Bombay. He thought the Congressmen were against us not because of Muslim catching reasons but because of ignorance of the problem. I should follow up the invitation of Irfan definitely. He wasn't a Zionist, but he would be ready to be in contact with London and Jerusalem, and to do everything here that we should feel is correct and possible. He knows Brodetski and Bentwich. He had a correspondence debate with Kallenbach in the *Jewish Chronicle* and *SA. Zionist Record* on the relationship of SA Jews to the Indians in Africa. The influence of Polak here was less because "we are tired of the so-called 'friends of India'"; but he anyway has a lot of good contacts with many influential Indians.

Sarojini, who is a very good friend of his, said to me once: "Polak is not like Kallenbach; he (Polak) makes money out of India".

14.9. Mr. Syed Abdulla Brelvi, editor of the *Bombay Chronicle*, Red Building, Parsi Bazaar Street, Fort Bombay, promises me to write an article in favour of an Arabic-Jewish conference. In the evening, to a performance of Harindranath Chattopadhyaya's operetta "Abdul-Hassan". At the end I had to step onto the stage at the request of Miss Chattopadhyaya and give garlands to the main actors and the author.

15.9. Visit to K.R. Kama, Oriental Institute, Sukhadwala Building, 172 Hornbey Road, Fort Bombay. The secretary, Mr. Behrangore T. Anklesaria, collects books for the library. Mr. Satyamurti asked in the house of Assembly an adjourment motion on the question of Palestine. The motion didn't get the permission of the Viceroy.

16.9. Sarojini gave me the following letters on the way:

1. to Mr. Lala Shankarlal, 20 Curzon Road, New Delhi. "My friend. Dr. O., a Jewish Savant from Palestine, is going to spend a few days in Delhi. He will arrive on Monday morning the 20th. He will wire you from Agra. Please meet him and show him every courtesy".
2. to Sir Shenmukham Chetty, Diwan of Cochin. "May I introduce my friend, Dr. O. of the Hebrew University of Palestine, who is going to be in Cochin for a few days in early October. He is making a study of the Jewish settlements in India. Please show him every courtesy and place some facilities in his way".

Over and above, she gave me another letter to Mrs. Hannah Sen, 1 Barakhamba Road, New Delhi. This is the wife of Dr. Sen, radiologist. She is half Jewish because her mother was a Jewess. She and her Hindu husband had visited Palestine. Her sister is married to a Muslim doctor in Hyderabad. Yesterday, 15.9, I wrote a serious letter to Brelvi where I said that opposition to murder shouldn't be voiced (as he has done in his Leader) because this justifies military occupation of the country, but because murder in itself is unacceptable. That's how students of Moses, Christ, Mohammad and Gandhi should think.

Today Brelvi rang up. He was quite concerned about my letter and wanted to talk to me. I told him I had no time because I was just about to leave. He asked me urgently at any rate to receive a reporter. Agreed. A young Hindu appeared, A.S. Iyer, Assistant Chief Reporter of the *Bombay Chronicle*. Detailed discussion about all the problems of Palestine for the newspaper as well as for his personal information. He doesn't share Brelvi's opinions; is an intelligent pro-Zionist Hindu. He was very impressed by my New Year's message to the Bene Israel, that they shouldn't with all their loyalty to Jewishness and to Palestine, neglect their Indian culture. Looking forward to what the *Bombay Chronicle* reports tomorrow. My earlier interviews with the Chronicle have been printed in full by the Associated Press Sarojini told me yesterday.

17.9. Today in the *Bombay Chronicle* printed under a banner headline "Zionist Terms for Peace in Palestine" recommending Arab-Jewish Conference without comment.

The Times of India brings a pro-Zionist interview of a Ahmed Safadi "an Arab farmer who arrived in Bombay from Palestine".

Brelvi writes me today he would like to have a detailed talk with me when I'm back on October 10th.

As I was driving in a car somebody called loudly my name in the middle of all the traffic. All the cars, mine included, had to stop. It was Sarojini who had seen me from her car. She stopped my car to tell me that she would recommend me by letter to a friend in Calcutta and I should give her my address in Calcutta so that she could send me a copy.

Mahadev Desai telegraphed a few days ago that Laemmel could receive me since he has recovered quite well.

Listening to the advice of Leser and some other friends I decided, at the last moment, to hire a boy for my long tour. I walked for half an hour up and down the street to find a one-day guide in Bombay. I finally found one—Siva-Hari—and hired him for 2 rupees a day, without any *bakshish*.

19.9. This morning Mahadev Desai expected me at the Wardha station and took me by car (which I had to pay for) to the ashram of Laemmel. A very weak Laemmel sat on his bed, just recovered from illness. On the floor sat 15 of his students. I got a place at the edge of the bed. I talked with him for about 20 minutes. I disliked the whole environment. But nobody could notice it. I told the Rebbe everything in detail. The Rebbe was silent and the students listened. He told me that Kallenbach had telegraphed and told him he would be with him by the end of October. He was looking very much forward to that letter. When I told him K. was a very active member of the S.A. Zionist Federation, he said: "I know! But then he has so many poor relatives". That's how he understands Zionism. I decided to let K. deal with this Goat-hero. When I realised that he really was very weak, I said goodbye. He struggled to get up but couldn't manage. He said very heartily goodbye and asked me to visit him once again if I was still in India when Kallenbach arrives.

On the way from Wardha to the ashram, Desai told me that the Arab High Committee had recently approached Laemmel and asked for his moral support.

On the way he bought at a druggist, Koramin and Adrenalin for Laemmel. Adrenalin! Well 'dem rebbens Kuh meg men'. I thought about what Chattopadhyaya told me later. Once the ashram was bothered by a lot of monkeys. "Monkeys on the trees, monkeys in the yard, monkeys here, monkeys there, monkeys, monkeys everywhere". Laemmel was very upset and ordered one monkey to be shot. Upset, one of the students asked: "But what about non-violence"? To which the Rebbe answered: "Well, non-violence as far as possible". Every surgical operation is, according to him forbidden, but he himself got his appendix removed.

A much bigger impression than he made on me I got of Khan Abdulghaffar Khan, the Frontier Gandhi, who I met here. He asked for all the details of the Zionist movement, talked with a lot of understanding for our part. He was in Palestine in 1926 and was very impressed by Tel Aviv. He met a lot of Jews and Arabs and recommended to both parties to learn from India and not let each other be stirred up against each other. He was very pleased about my interview with the *Bombay Chronicle* and the suggestion of an Arab-Jewish Conference. He agreed with this idea and wanted to support it.

In the ashram: a school, a Hindu temple where there is no immorality as Desai said with pride, and a leather factory. The head of this factory is a Brahmin. He wants to start trade relations with P. and believes he can beat any competition from

Czechoslovakia because, as he declares with beaming eyes, his workers are willing to work for 2 annas a day.

In the afternoon at Bajaj, a millionaire, who lives very modestly and supports Congress (because of the 2 annas of course). His son Ram Krishna writes to my Gideon for stamps. Meet Rajendra Prasad,[24] former Congress president there. All sit in a narrow row on a long white towel. In front of everybody a bowl from which they eat with their hands. I sit on a chair at a table and eat with a spoon, fork and knife, buttermilk, cucumber, butter, tea. I started to eat. Suddenly I realise that Prasad is chanting something. I apologise for not knowing the foreign habits which (the apology) brings me immediately close to them. As they ask, I tell them about our eating habits and they find the "Hammozi lechem"[25] and "Baruch sheechalnu mishelo"[26] very beautiful. I repeated the words a few times with their kind acceptance. I told a lot more about Palestine and had to answer many questions, and I got the distinct impression that Prasad didn't agree with Nehru's attitude and would like the Congress to be totally neutral.

Before I left for Delhi, I had to wait for about one hour at Wardha station. One of the disciples appeared to "bid me goodbye". He said: "A pity you did not talk longer to him. You speak so convincingly. We were all very much interested". There formed a bigger circle of Congressmen from this area which is full of them, and I was assailed with questions. Everybody showed great interest and accepted my pro-Zionist arguments with sympathy.

Earlier I sat on a bench with many others. Siva-Hari came up and said: "It is a dull place Wardha, sir". To which I replied: "There is only one Wardha in the world, because there is only one G. in the world" (which is true and expressed my mood at that moment). A happy look in the eyes of the Indians, joy about the recognition from the side of a European.

21.9. Arrived in Delhi today. Phoned Dr. Hannah Sen. Her husband invited me immediately to dinner. He was angry that the boy who he took to the station could not find me. And then

---

24. Later President of India.
25. Blessing before breaking bread.
26. Blessing after the meal.

he said: "It was cruel of Dr. Sen to take you away from me". I should go immediately to him, should actually be his guest and live with him. I appeared soon in his luxurious house to which he had already invited a journalist. He also led me to his brother, Shri Ram, who was also unbelievably obliging. They had total understanding for Zionism and were glad to hear more details from me. They complained that nothing was done from the Jewish side to introduce the Jewish point of view to the Indian public. Such information as mine could not fail to impress both Hindus and Muslims in a positive way. I shouldn't go to Aligarh because the university had holidays and was closed.

Once at Sarojini's in Bombay I got to know Prof. K.G. Saijidin from the University of Aligarh. Together with him there was also Miss S. Ram, Lady Hardinge Medical College, 96 Lady Hardinge Road.

Dr. and Mrs. Sen had both been in Palestine in 1926. They knew Miss Szold. The mother of Mrs. Sen was born Gubbay from Palestine. I met there a Lal, who works in the local _Statesman_ (Delhi), together with a certain Mr. Jacobsen who will interview me tomorrow. I also met at Sen's Mrs. Nehru, a cousin of Jawaharlal's, who inquired in detail about everything and showed great understanding and enthusiasm about my explanation of Zionism. She is leading here a Harijan colony that is in contact with Congress. She can now, after I explained things to her, not forgive Jawaharlal that he was talking about things he didn't know enough about.

In the afternoon the Sens took me to the inauguration party of the house of a rich Indian. I talked to many Indians, some Muslims.

Mrs. Ram invited me for supper.

Mr. Ashik Ahmed (_The Statesman_, New Delhi) saw me today to interview me for the newspaper. Later he came again for further additions and explanations. He is Muslim, but shares fully our position. We shouldn't believe that all Muslims are like the Shaukat group.

Together with him I visited Mr. S. Jacobsen, _The Statesman_, New Delhi. Jacobsen's mother had informed him from London that I would be in India and he expected me with impatience. My intention not to go to Simla. He promised to write to El Epstein to tell him about his own opinion about India-Palestine and offered to be available for us on the whole should Jerusalem ask him to.

In the afternoon I drove with Mrs. Nehru to the Harijan school (Harijan, that is, God's children, a name Gandhi coined, and that now is commonly used for the Untouchables). The leaders gave me material for the library and promised to send me more. At 4.30, a lecture in the Lady Hardinge College. Mrs. Nehru was present and S. Ram led the assembly. Big applause. Also on the way to the hotel of Mrs. Nehru, Shankarlal took my address in case he would come to Palestine.

22.9. 7 o'clock in the evening the train to Allahabad. Alliance Hotel. Phoned immediately to Nehru whose sister was very pleased and invited me to tea at 4.

I utilised the time in between to visit the university where I met first the Rector (Vice-Chancellor, because the office of a Chancellor in all universities in India is an honorary post either filled by a Governor or a Maharajah), Pandit Iqbal Narain Gurtu; and secondly to meet again my pal from the sea journey, Prof Mitter. Pandit Gurtu, M.A., LLB, was honoured, assured his sympathies for us, and asked his personal assistant, P.I. Das, to show me the university. He promised to send a list of the extra copies of the library to Jerusalem in exchange for any duplicates of our library. Dr. J. Mitter (Botanic) was very pleased when he saw me and introduced me to his colleague Dr. S. Ranjan. I had to tell about our university, the faculties, and position of Botany. I gave them the address of Reubenis to whom they will suggest to exchange plant collections. I should talk to Reubeni about it. Ranjan intends to visit Palestine in May 1937 and noted my address down. Dr. Mitter called immediately for an assembly in the Botanical Institute for 3 p.m. The Polish-Jewish teacher of French and German should attend that too (she is married to a Hindu). Her name is Mrs. Kali; before it was Miss Simeon Teck. All teachers and about 70 students came to the assembly, among them some Muslims. Dr. S. Ranjan was in the chair and he found very warm words for Zionism. Well received lecture and answers. Ranjan gave me a letter of recommendation for his brother Shri Nandan, Benaras Motor Works, Benaras.

At 4 p.m. at Nehru's who had invited guests. Rich house, European, where inhabitants and guests, as everywhere in India,

walk barefoot. Nehru's only agrument—Imperialism. Among
other things he said "Zionism is a movement of Jewish high
finance, is it not"? When I denied that vehemently and told him
and the persons present the nature of Zionism, it was a Sinai
revelation for them. Nehru said he was opposed to any
imperialism whether British or Hitlerite. To my remark that in
Palestine one says that Hitler supports the Arabs, he said: "We
have sympathy for the national movement of the Arabs in
Palestine because this movement opposes British Imperialism.
Our sympathies cannot be diminished by the fact that the
nationalist Arab movement coincides with Hitler's interests".
Then me: "Didn't you just say that you opposed any
imperialism? But the Arab nationalist movement doesn't lose
anything in your eyes. You could say with the same justification:
we are sympathetic to the nationalist movement of the Jews and
that this movement coincides with the interests of England
doesn't change our sympathy". He was a bit embarrassed. I used
the situation and said: "But, of course, there are not 70,000,000
Jews in India". Then he said something like, "I understand the
Jewish problem, but it can only be solved when in the big fight
between Fascism and Socialism, the latter succeeds. This fight
can last for generations". I said: "Fight between Fascism and
Socialism! In your eyes, is Hitler fighting on the side of
Socialism? This fight could last for generations and we should
wait patiently till then. You know whom I feel like here as a
representative of the Jews? You tell me: 'Dear friend, you are
very nice but you have to die. I'm very sorry about it, but I can't
help it. Drink your cup of tea and be so kind as to die' ". All
present laughed and he too. In the course of the discussion he
said: "Naturally we condemn the riots and atrocities!" Me: "A
pity the Arabs never heard you condemn it". He: "Well, if they
did not, they are going to; you can be sure of that. We are trying
at present to explain to the Muslims here that the fight in P. is not
one between Jews and Arabs, but between both and British
Imperialism; and that they should not protest against Jews but
against the British Government which hinders the development
of peaceful relations". A brother-in-law of Nehru's, who was
present, is specifically pro-Zionist. He addressed a writing in this
spirit to the Palestine Conference. He promised me to send a
copy to Arakie, Calcutta.

What was new to everybody including Nehru, was my description of the Kibbutzim—something they thought almost unbelievable.

Dr. Ranjan's letter to his brother in Benaras is as follows: "The bearer of this, Dr O., is from Palestine. He is connected with the Hebrew University there and other cultural activities. If you can spare a few hours and take him to a few learned people, it will be nice".

23.9. Today appears in the morning press as a morning greeting an appeal by Nehru for Palestine Day which is arranged for 27.9—sympathy for the gallant people struggling for freedom.

In Benaras my first visit takes me to the ill Soc., Narendra Devh, who I met in Bombay. I went to him along with Lohia, Secretary of Congress, who had left together with me from Allahabad. He was grateful for the visit. Engaged discussion. He admires the Kibbutzim; doubts their continuation through several generations. The young Lohia is here the expert on foreign affairs because he was seven years in America and knows the "Affairs of the World" almost as well as Nehru. His stay in America convinced him that the Jews weren't a people at all and would soon be absorbed by other people. Antisemitism was only a "passing phase", etc. The main argument or rather the only argument against us by Devh was again imperialism.

About Laemmel they tell all kind of things. Some talk about him as a saint who can heal the sick and perform miracles. Others maintain he had, when he worked together with Shaukat[27], made lakhs of rupees. His friendship with the half-mad Annie Besant[28] is mentioned with a significant smile. Others maintain he is working for Amalek.[29] Nothing surprises me.

Visit at the Vice-Chancellor of the Hindu University of Benaras, Pandit M.M. Malaviya. He was radiant, happy that I honoured him with my visit; promised to send publications to the university of Jerusalem and is, though a Congressman, convinced of the desirable victory of Zionism. I should write to

---

27. He supported the Mufti in organising the World Islamic Conference.
28. A theosophist who was a prominent figure in the early years of the Indian nationalist movement.
29. A people who attacked the Children of Israel during their wanderings in the desert at the time of Moses. Now come to mean an antisemite.

him about the student exchange between Benaras and Jerusalem even though, at the moment, he couldn't decide anything. He could see the beauty of the idea of reviving the relationship between Palestine (Jews) and India.

24.9.   Arrived today in Calcutta. Found a letter from Sarojini to Ramanand Chatterji, Editor of *The Modern Review*, Calcutta. I visited him immediately and found an old man who also was ill. He knows about the topic, regrets and complains that there is no Zionist propaganda here. He will get me the necessary connections even though he cannot leave the house because of his illness.

This morning the Chairman of the Calcutta group of the Congress Socialists rang me up to talk at the Palestine Day. I explained I couldn't do it.

25.9.   Last night at 6, lecture in the enormous house of Curlender. About 95 people present among others, Dr. Meytra, who was in P. about a year ago taking part in the congress of doctors. Supports us totally. He nodded in agreement to everyone of my sentences but had to leave 15 min. before the end in order to catch a train. I met him again after a few days. According to his opinion the newspapers here—the English and Indian ones—should be bombarded with articles because, especially the Indian Press, could only be influenced by that.

I was at *The Statesman* today, to visit editor Moor, who was contacted by Jacobsen from Delhi, but I wasn't allowed to see him because I refused to say "on what business" I wanted to see him. I wrote him a few lines to explain the problem and left. After half-an-hour I got a letter through a courier where he apologised and asked me to see him again.

I was visited by students Banerji and Das Gupta, representing the Nationalist Party, with a writing from their President, D. Dakrawat, by order of Chatterji (through Sarojini): it was decided to give a lecture about Palestine at the Calcutta University Institute; later one about art.

Dr. S.K. Chatterji (15 Hindustan Road) rang me back at 8 o'clock and is going to visit me at 10 tomorrow. He has written pro-Jewish articles in *The Modern Review* where he is working under Ramanand Chatterji. All that he explained to me on the phone.

Moor from *The Stateman,* who I visited this afternoon, thinks that after all he has seen last year in Palestine (and what he also reported about in *The Times*) that our success is secured. He also believes that the Muslims here are being ignored by the Jewish side. It's a bad idea, because their opposition isn't only based on anti-government motives but also as a result of the Arab propaganda (which is not corrected by the Jewish side) that the Jews in Palestine are pushing out the Arabs. I definitely should talk to Abdul Ali, which also the Zionists here recommend.

The two students who visited me also complained about a lack of information from the Jewish side.

Tomorrow, Sunday 27th, an appointment with K.S. Roy, Secretary of Bengal Provincial Congress Committee.

Prof. Suniti Kumar Chatterji, M.A., D. Litt., linguist at the university, Calcutta (Sudharma, 16 Hindustan Park, Boliganj, Calcutta) was here. Took some literature. He also complained that the Indians hear only one point of view. At 1 o'clock we drove together to the university where we, together with Prof. S. Mookerjee, discussed a lecture for the 30th. I also met a Muslim scholar, Schoffen (student of Prof. Horowitz, Frankfort, later Aligarh) who is pro-Zionist and wants to try to get me to meet people like him.

Wrote to Jerusalem about Prof. Julius Bloch (*Veda aux temps modernes,* Paris, 1934). Also about the bad influence Sylvan Levy has had here.

28.9. This afternoon I got a visit by J. Nayogi (1/5 Raja Dinendra Street) of the Bengal Provincial Committee and at the same time representative of the Commercial Museum, Corporation of Calcutta. He came with his colleague by order of Roy who was ill. He was pleased with my deliberation. The Congress people in Bengal were supporting the Jewish demands.

Got letters from Jawahar and Desai. Jawahar shows embarrassment.

Prof. Dr. Levi, 6 Old Post Office Street, invited me to dinner, and Dr. Treu for another day.

Hofmeyer arrived with the South African delegation in Calcutta.

I visited him in his "Great Eastern" hotel. He was glad to see me again. Reported about the good results of the KH-action in

South Africa; praised Brodetski and Mrs. Sieff; and asked about the events in Palestine. The African government was always ready to help us.

At 6 in the evening, lecture at the Calcutta University Institute under the chairmanship of T.C. Goswani, Barrister-at-law (address above). Good attention and general applause. Goswani admitted that until now he had not understood the whole question. Now he is completely convinced. It was difficult in India to say anything against the Arab demands because the Muslims would immediately say "offending Islam".

The students force me to talk about Art on October 2nd.

The Harijan Sangh in Delhi owns a fund called David Scholarship. When I inquired, the head of the Sangh told me that this was in honour of a Jewish merchant from Bombay who donated the first Rs. 2500. In March 1935, the fund was renamed and is now called "Gandhiji Educational Scholarship". !30

1.10. The lecture for the Council of Professors became a big assembly attended by professors and students. Most of the professors heard about the Jewish point of view for the first time. There were also Muslim students present. I talked with care and tact which everybody acknowledged. In the afternoon at S.K. Chatterji to tea, where philologists attended. A "mad" philologist head; knows a lot. Over the entrance a hexagon, like the *swastika*, a holy symbol of Hinduism. I said: one has been adopted by the Jews, the other by the Nazis. He laughed. Over all the doors and wherever there is place in the walls, sentences in all kind of languages. Among others in old Hebrew writing:

---

30. Unfortunately the General Secretary of the Harijan Sevak Sangh who wrote to Olsvanger did not give the initial or first name of David so one is at a loss to know which particular David is referred to. The most likely candidate is E.D. David. The following quotation is taken from the Fischel papers in the possession of the late Mrs. Shirley Berry Isenberg:

"Mr. E.D. David belongs to an old Jewish family that settled down in British Cochin. He has travelled abroad and among the places he visited is Eretz Israel. Mr. David takes a keen interest in the education of Jewish students and is the originator of the Jewish Friend In Need Society, the principal aim of which is to supply poor students with books and their fees. Mr. David is also a liberal giver to Jewish and other charities".

(Thanks to Drs. Chaya Brasz, Director of the Centre of Research on Dutch Jewry at the Hebrew University of Jerusalem, for allowing the papers to be lodged there when they were being scrutinized).

"Elohi, lama asawtani".[31]   I told them about the revival of Hebrew, the changes in syntax, and much else. In view of the language question in India and the quiet attempt to revive Sanskrit, they found everything very interesting.

In the evening Chatterji took me to a theatre performance in classical Sanskrit to a totally packed theatre.

Rai Som Narayan Sinha (Cawnpore U.P., Zoder, Santiniketan), who I met on the train on my way to Tagore, asks me to contact him as soon as I return to Palestine, to send him material and to stay in contact with him. The Director of Santiniketan leads me to the aged Tagore who greets me Indian style. He doesn't remember our conversation in Bucharest. He repeats he is a warm friend of Zionism; regrets that he never could visit Palestine; and that travelling was difficult now at the age of 76. He always hoped that Jews and Arabs could build a "Palestine nationality" and it gives him pain that this should be so difficult. He is certainly hoping that the Arabs one day will appreciate the influx of Jews in every way. He was sorry about Nehru's tactics, based on internal Indian interests, which are also rather bad for India itself. He said very heartily goodbye by taking my hands into his. The Director bowed deeply and wiped the dust off his feet as is demanded by the difference in age and caste.

I had to type the interview for the Director on a typewriter. He added Tagore's opinions.[32]

On the way back I drove for some time with Sinha. He regretted never to have heard about Zionism, this Zionism. He advised me to visit P.C. Roy in Calcutta, though he isn't in India at the moment.

2.10.   Prof. Benoy Kumar Sarkar, national economist, was the chairman of the assembly of the Radical Students Union where I talked about "Art: individual and collective". At the end of the lecture he said: "This lecture will long be remembered on the

---

31. My God, why hast thou forsaken me (Psalm 22).
32. The Olvanger papers contain a letter dated October 23, 1936, from Tagore's Secretary, Anil K. Chanda. One paragraph reads as follows:
    "The Vishva-Bharati Publishing Board which owns the Bengali works to the Poet, has been asked to send a set of his Bengali books to the Hebrew University Library in Jerusalem, as requested by you".
    Another scholastic coup by Olsvanger.

shores of the Ganges". In the introduction he spoke warmly about Jews and Judaism and the rebirth of Israel happening at this moment. Prof. Guha (Zoological Survey of India, India Museum, Calcutta; Telegr. Adr. Zoology; telephone: Regent 513 Calcutta) and Dr. D.N. Maitra (4, Sambhunath Street, P.O. Elgin Road, Calcutta, telephone: Park 900) were present. Prof. Guha and his colleagues would like to be in contact with our university, especially Archaeology, and they plan to visit Palestine. Maitra thought one should work on the press here systematically and shouldn't shun work or expense.

The reporter of *The Advance* took a detailed interview which he will distribute through the Associated Press. Also the Santiniketan interview is going through the Ass. Press.

Guha recommends me to a colleague of his at the A. Aiyatfan Museum, Madras: "I am introducing Dr. I.O. of the Hebrew University in Jerusalem, a very distinguished scholar. He is on a short visit to India. He is leaving for Madras tomorrow and will reach there on Monday. He will spend the day in Madras and take the evening train to Cochin. I shall be much obliged if you show him round the city and other things in which he might be interested".

Mr. B Berkhoff, 32 Dalhousie Square, Calcutta, asks for detailed literature about P. (English). He is an English Jew, young merchant with good Indian connections.

Also Dr. F. Greilsamer, Maisel and Co. Ltd., P.O.B. 2164, Calcutta, asks for some. He agrees to help and to correspond with the main office. He recommends talking to Herrn Walter Wolff, P.O.B. 1259, Haifa, who knows India well, and has, like his wife, good connections here. The sister of Chattopadhyaya also asked me to give her regards to the Wolffs.

In the evening I visit Dr. Ghosh whose wife was born Wilbuschewitz from Bjalostok daughter of Ewgeni Wilbuschewitz. Both Zionists. They told me about the strong Hitler propaganda in India. There exists an Indian Association in Calcutta "Society of Friends of New Germany". I was told by someone else that the Congress movement is directly supported from there. Most people I asked deny such a possibility.

Ghosh from Santiniketan, who unfortunately I couldn't meet, wrote after his visit to Palestine friendly articles in the local Bengali newspaper.

Mr. Amiruddin Ahmed, Advocate, Calcutta High Court (51, Alimuddin Street, Calcutta), was my companion on the 24 hour journey from Calcutta to Madras. He thanked me for previous information on Palestine. Asks permission to correspond and for literature.

4.10. Madras. I didn't meet the colleague at the Aiyatfan Museum to whom Dr. Guha has recommended me. Instead I met the assistant, M.D. Raghavan, with whom I talked in the presence of his colleagues for over an hour. Everything was new to them. Raghavan asked me urgently for literature. Agreed to talk to the Mayor on my return from Cochin.

6.10. Arrived in Ernaculum. At the station, besides Salem and Koder, a representative of the State, since I was (as Salem tells me) a guest of the State. A lot of "black" and "white" Jews have come to the station. They gave me a golden garland according to Indian tradition and greeted me with "shalom". From there we sailed in the state boat to Cochin to the "Malabar" hotel. This hotel is on an island that has been reclaimed from the sea and is about 3–4 sq. km. The huge Malabar bay, lined by green woods, is enchanting. This is the biggest future harbour of India from which direct connections to Europe, Egypt, and Palestine will be arranged—"Zdyessey budyet gorod zalozhon"!—and a big town in 4–5 years.

In the afternoon the whole community of Cochin came to the assembly, enlarged by the Jewish group from Ernaculum who got free boats for the occasion. I had a strong pain in my ear, but I forgot the pain at the strange sight of this new type of Jew who, like the Bene Israel, have thousands of years of Indian history behind them.

At the assembly I learned of Dizengoff's death.[33]

The chairman was a Hindu, Mr. M.S. Menon. His introductory and finishing words astounded me with his knowledge of the problem; his honest appreciation of Judaism; and his conviction of the success of our work in P. The representatives of the *Madras Mail* and *The Hindu* (Madras) told me that they heard for the first time the Jewish point of view from a representative; the one from *The Hindu* assured me that he had changed his point of view basically in our favour.

---

33. Mayor of Tel Aviv.

The "Manifesto" of the Congress of 25.9 much milder than Jawahar's statement to the press.

For literature and correspondence request:

T.M. Satchit, journalist, editor, *Cochin Argus*, Cochin News Agency, Rajalakshmi & Co (specially about Kibbutzim);

K.B. Menon, Editor, *Cochin Chronicle*.

Visit to the Diwan, Sir Shenmukham Chetty. Over one hour intense discussion. It was new to him that one talked Hebrew in P. He intends to visit the country and takes my address down.

Unfortunately the Maharajah is not present, but he will convey my greetings. The Maharajah is a Sanskrit scholar, but he doesn't speak any other language but this and Malayalam.

Salem and Koder receive my suggestion about a trade agreement with Cochin seriously and want to discuss the details with the Diwan; then they will let me know.

When I had to leave for the train, two representatives of the State accompanied me and we discussed the suggestions for the contract. They both thought it was possible to carry it out.

8.10. In Madras I was asked by the Editor of the *Madras Mail* for a detailed interview. I also visited the Muslim Mayor of the town, Abdul Hamed Khan. He goes in for an Arab-Jewish conference; believes in the possibility of mutual understanding; and was honoured by my visit.

On my way to Bombay, talked in the train to Mr. K.R. Gunjikar, Royal Institute of Science, Bombay.

12.10. In Poona visit to the "Servants of India Society" that has 30 members in the whole country and is organising and leading cultural and economical activities.

15.10. Visit to the Kama Oriental Institute. Anklesaria has given me a beautiful collection of this Institute as well as the Kama Athornan Institute. He also recommended me to the Iranian League. The Secretary of the League, Mr Kaikhosrow A. Fitter (Iranian League, Naswari Buildings, Hornby Road, Fort Bombay) asked me for literature about the colonisation. He is excited about the idea of a renewal of the relationship between India and Palestine. He is very worried about the situation in the government. The Agency should do something in this direction. That could also win the sympathies of the Persian Muslims.

18.10. Visit to the art collector Treasurywalla (5, Club Road, Byculla, Bombay). Long talk about P. and Zionism.

21.10. Second visit to Buniyad Huseinkhan Bundukhan (Bombay Minerva Films, Siwry Bombay). He is leader of a music school; Muslim. Wants to go to Palestine with his orchestra to give concerts. In his school I met for the first time Irfan.

23.10. Salem reports from Cochin that he has talked to the Diwan who is positive about the plan for a contract.

25.10. Assembly in Ahmedabad under the chairmanship of the Parsi doctor, Col. Sir B.H. Nanawati, CIE, FRCS. Mixed audience—Jews, Muslims, Hindus and Parsis. Undoubted success with everybody. The introductory words of the chairman as well as the final address of a Parsi professor—very satisfactory.

Visit with Dr. Benjamin (Bene Israel) at the Muslim leader, Sir Mahabubmiys Kadri, friend of the Jews and of Zionism, who intends to come to Palestine.

At Sarabhai's, one of the richest mill-owners and a Congressman, for dinner. About 30 guests, family members and friends. Unfortunately the father was travelling, but I will meet him tomorrow at the theatre.

Bharati Sarabhai, who I knew from the boat, said: "The attitude of the Congress on the Palestine Question is due to tactical reasons". To which I answered: "Tell me, Miss Bharati, imagine if it were in the interest of the Jews in Palestine for tactical reasons to oppose your Congress. What would you say if the Jews would call a meeting in Jerusalem under the name "India Day" and pass resolutions against Congress? What would you say?" Everybody was embarrassed. I used this embarrassment and said gravely: "My friends, there should be such a thing as morals even in politics, and one should not play politics with human misery". We talked until late at night in the overly luxurious, beautiful garden, and the young people couldn't get enough of the information I gave them. Miss Nalini N. Jaykrishnadas (18 years old), Vasant Vihar, Shahibag, Ahmedabad, wants to correspond with a girl or a boy of the same age in Palestine.

29.10. Pandit Narayanrao Vyas, Gayanacharya, Vyas Bhuvan, 148, Hindu Colony, Dadar, Bombay, intends perhaps to visit Palestine to give Indian concerts.

From Ahmedabad I intend to take a train to Bombay. Because the day journey is so tiring, I have called a Zionist Assembly for the next evening in Bombay. I stayed overnight as I wanted to see the performance of Chattopadhyaya, a brother of Sarojini. He himself is important. Also.I wanted to get to know Sarabhai. When Sarabhai's children drew his attention to me, he came to me and greeted me like an old friend. He only had one criticism of Zionism: the Jews were bringing a European way of life to Asia,

Appendix-1

Addres :

    c/o India League
    165 Strand
    London W.C.2

Highgate (London)
3.9. 36

Dear Dr Olsvanger,

    Thank you for your letters. I would love to visit Palestine but what can one do there when bombs are being thrown daily on innocent people and martial law prevails. What a terrible time that unfortunate country is having and there seems no prospect of peace. I am more certain than ever that these two communities tenacious and bully each other will never arrive only way to find a solution of this problem is Arabs and Jews to meet and confer together and agree. To rely on British authorities is to court failure.

    I had the good fortune to meet Dr Weizmann in London.

Yours sincerely

Jawaharlal Nehru

ALL INDIA CONGRESS COMMITTEE
SWARAJ BHAWAN-ALLAHABAD

OFFICE BEARERS FOR 1936
President:
   Jawaharlal Nehru
Treasurer:
   Jamnalal Bajaj
General Secretary:
   J. B. Kripalani

Telephone: 341
Telegrams: "Congress"
Ref.

August 29, 1936

Dear Dr. Olsvanger,

    I received your letter as I was leaving Bombay. I read it with great interest. I am very glad that I have had an opportunity of meeting you and of learning much from you. This will certainly help me to form a clear opinion about events in Palestine. I shall be very glad if you could arrange to send me literature on the subject. This will be appreciated by our office also.

    I am writing to you briefly today as I have to face a great deal of work on my return here. I hope that if you come this way we shall meet again.

Sincerely Yours,

Jawaharlal Nehru

Dr. Immanuel Olsvanger,
The Ritz Hotel,
Bombay.

4 ZALMAN SHAZAR AVE
POSTAL ADDRESS. P.O.B. 92
JERUSALEM 91020
PHONE 820155
FAX 827029

הארכיון הציוני המרכזי
CENTRAL ZIONIST ARCHIVES

ALL INDIA CONGRESS COMMITTEE
SWARAJ BHAWAN-ALLAHABAD

OFFICE BEARERS FOR 1936
President:
  Jawaharlal Nehru
Treasurer:
  Jamnalal Bajaj
General Secretary:
  J. B. Kripalani

Telephone: 341
Telegrams: "Congress"
Ref. G5/2201

September 25, 1936

Dr. I. Olsvanger*,
c/o E.A. Araki, M.A., JP.
50, Bowbazaar St.
Calcutta

Dear Dr. Olsvanger,

I have received your letter. The statement you refer to was issued some days ago, probably the day before I saw you. I am afraid we are not likely to convert each other completely. We approach the question from different view-points. But, at any rate, we need not suspect the good faith of the other. It seems to me that you have not done me the courtesy in believing in my bona fides. So far as I am concerned politics and morals have seldom drifted far apart and I have tried to act publicly in the Congress with my conception of morality. I believe in every word of what I have said in regard to Palestine. I may change that belief

---

* This is a reply to my (Olsvanger's) letter criticising N's statement to the press. The copy of this letter got lost (stolen!).

with further knowledge but with all deference to you my knowledge of the world situation is not insignificant. I hold that it is impossible to understand any problem, whether that of India or Palestine, without reference to that larger situation and I hold that the Arab movement is essentially a nationalist movement, though there are certain complicating factors like relics of feudalism etc. The fact that ignorant or mischievous Arabs have been misbehaving cannot take away from the essential character of that movement. It astonishes me for you to tell me that I am siding with the enemies of freedom in Palestine. In my recent statement I mentioned the large additions to British troops that are being sent to Palestine. I suppose, according to you, these British troops are the friends of freedom in Palestine. I hold differently.

As I dictate this letter my office is being searched by a crowd of police men under the orders of the local magistrate. This is a gentle reminder to me of how imperialism functions in this country. I cannot tolerate this imperialism in India or Palestine and the question I ask every one is whether he stands for this imperialism or against it.

Yours sincerely

Jawaharlal Nehru

CZA/S25/3583

S25/3583

Calcutta, 28.9.36.
c/o E.A. Arakie, M.A., JP.
50, Bowbazaar Street.

Pandit Jawaharlal Nehru
Allahabad.

Dear Pandit Nehru,

I thank you for your letter of Sept. the 25th. In my last letter to you I used a turn of speech which I afterwards regretted. It was not well chosen, and I beg of you to excuse me. I certainly had not in my mind any doubt of the sincerety of your views. But when I said, that "morals and politics do not go hand in hand"— I wanted to say, that very often a political attitude, which is predominant in a person hinders that person from seeing certain negative moments in an event that seems to serve his main political interests.

I never doubted that your "knowledge of the world's situation is not insignificant". Neither did I in my letter to you give expression to such a doubt. Believe me that I entertain a great admiration for your knowledge, your learning and the nobility of your character. But your knowledge about conditions in Palestine is very much incomplete and onesided. In your speech at Allahabad yesterday you deplored" some excesses and follies of Arabs and Jews". Some? Is that right? I refuse to believe that this statement came from your soul. Is deploring all that you could find to say? Is not the strongest condemnation called for? You write that ignorant and mischievous Arabs have been misbehaving. It was not that. It was criminal organised murder in the service of feudalism. One day you will see it. One day you will also see, which form the gratitude of those whom you support will accept. A national movement? So the leaders of the revolution in Spain say about the unfortunate millions who fight to their own detriment against the Spanish government of to-day.

But you deplored in your speech "some excesses and follies of Arabs *and Jews*". What excesses and follies have Jews in Palestine committed? On the strength of what evidence do you throw this accusation against the Jews of Palestine? I was gallant enough to give you for your information the address of the paper of our enemies. But do you implicitly believe all calumnies coming from that or similar sources? Does not elementary justice require to verify press-statements before accusing people of crime and murder? Not one act of atrocities has been committed by Jews in Palestine.

The "Falastin", an Arab paper in Palestine, a few weeks ago brought the news, that signatures are being collected in some Arab villages under a petition of protest against the cessation of Jewish immigration into Palestine. Why do these Arab villages do that? For the love of the Jews? Or are they bribed by the Jews? Or is it on the inspiration of the Government? No. It is because they know what stoppage of immigration would mean for them: loss of means of existence, loss of freedom, the return under the power of those who all these months agitated them against us Jews. These villagers think of their freedom. But you through your press statement to the press and your speech at Allahabad did side with the enemies of their freedom. The question of British politics is not affected by this problem. However the question of Jewish-Arab cooperation will be solved—Britain will continue her policy there.

Please, compare the situation in Palestine to-day and that in Transjordan. Whilst in Palestine, owing to the labour of the Jews, the standard of life of the whole population rose to undreamt of heights—the population of Transjordan remained in misery and poverty, so that about 20,000 of them emigrated to Palestine, finding employment with Jews and Arabs. If Jews were allowed to go into Transjordan they would in the course of a few years transform the whole aspect and life of that part of Palestine. But they are not allowed to do so. Because neither the British Government *nor yourself* would permit it. In that you would agree with British policy.

But why so much writing and talking? Would not you one day come over to Palestine and study the problem on the spot. I assure you of a most cordial and warm reception. I promise you one thing more. I will introduce you not only to all leading men and women of the Jewish work, but equally to prominent Arabs, who are leading the agitation against us. It is my sincerest desire that you should gather informations from all sides separately. After that I would love to have another talk with you.

With best regards
Yours sincerely
(Olsvanger)

4 ZALMAN SHAZAR AVE
POSTAL ADDRESS. P.O.B. 92
JERUSALEM 91920
PHONE 820155
FAX 827029

האָרכיון הציוני הַמֶרכזי
CENTRAL ZIONIST ARCHIVES

שד' זלמן שזר 4
מען למכתבים: ת"ד 92
ירושלים 91920
טלפון 820155
פקס 827029

41331. aleph

As at Anand Bhawan
Allahabad, February 2, 1938

Dear Dr. Olsvanger,

I am grateful to you for your message of sympathy.

I do not remember if I thanked you for sending me a copy of the Round Table containing an article on Palestine. I read this article with interest and I have been trying to follow developments in Palestine with some care. I must confess that I am distressed at what is happening there and I see no way out of this tangle by the method that the British Government is pursuing. I wish the Jews did not rely so much on the British Government and would seek a settlement directly with the Arabs. That would be both honourable and lasting. Any other attempt at a settlement will fail and will bring greater bitterness in its train.

Sincerely yours

Jawaharlal Nehru

Dr. J. Olsvanger
77, Great Russell Street,
London W.C. 1

41332-aleph

As from: 17 York Road,
New Delhi
22 May 1947

Dear Dr. Olsvanger,

Thank you for your letter dated 19th April which I received some time ago. I enclose a copy of a letter I am sending to Mr. Ben-Tow. I received your previous letter also. I was not hurt by it, of course, but I felt sad. We are all struggling through very difficult times and sometimes the light is dim. Nevertheless we try to follow that light to the best of our ability.

Yours sincerely

Jawaharlal Nehru

Encl: 1

41333-aleph

No. 437–PMH/54
New Delhi,
June 10, 1954.

Dear Dr. Olsvanger,

Thank you for your letter of the 27th May.
I was glad to hear from you.

I am interested to know about the activities of Indian Jews who have migrated from India to Israel.

You ask me for a message for a conference. Being Prime Minister and Foreign Minister, I have to restrain myself in regard to sending messages, because sometimes all kinds of meanings are attached to them. More especially at this rather critical juncture in the world's history, I try to be as silent as I can be. There is far too much talk indulged in by the tribe of politicians of which I am a very talkative member. So you will excuse me.

I am glad to learn that you have translated some of the stories of the Mahabharata into Hebrew.

With all good wishes.

Yours very sincerely

Jawaharlal Nehru

Dr. I. Olsvanger,
3 Gaza Road,
Jerusalem, Israel.

הארכיון הציוני המרכזי
CENTRAL ZIONIST ARCHIVES

41334-aleph

No. 2499-PMH/56
New Delhi,
October 16, 1956

Dear Dr. Olsvanger,

Thank you for your letter of the 4th October and your translation of the Bhagwad Gita. I am grateful to you for sending this book. I am afraid I am unable to read it and profit by it. But, I am happy that the Gita has been translated into Hebrew.

Yours sincerely

Jawaharlal Nehru

Dr. I. Olsvanger,
3 Gaza Road,
Jerusalem, Israel

CONFIDENTIAL & PERSONAL

No. 662-PMH/58.

New Delhi,
March 23, 1958.

Dear Dr. Olsvanger,

I have today received your letter. I have read about your dream and your visions about the coming of the inter-planetary age. Thank you for it. I have no doubt that the next few years will see great developments, not only in the inter-planetary sense, but in the impact of this new dimension on human beings, that is, if human beings are not too stupid. Anyhow the impact will be there, whether we are wise or stupid.

Sometimes I feel that all our arguments about present-day problems are rather out-of-date and indicate the enormous hiatus between our politics and men's thinking and the new world that is gradually taking shape. And yet the problems of today bear down upon us. We cannot ignore them and take refuge in the future.

You know well our attitude to Israel and our difficulties. We have never been unfriendly to Israel, though we have not always approved of what it has done. We earnestly hope that these problems will be solved peacefully and cooperatively. How can we help in this? I have felt and I still feel that we cannot be helpful just by sending an Ambassador to Israel.

I do not remember saying anywhere that Israel was a foreign body in the family of Asian nations. I may have said that Israel has looked to Europe and America more than to Asia, and it has therefore not fitted in with Asia. But what is Asia? I suppose there is something about the Asian concept, but it is vague and incapable of definition. There is vast variety in this great continent.

The inter-planetary age will come in, but perhaps you and I may not see it bloom. You will soon be 70 and I am very near your age. In another twenty months I shall be 70.

All good wishes on the anniversary of your birth.

Yours sincerely

Jawaharlal Nehru

Dr. I. Olsvanger,
5 Gaza Road,
Jerusalem, Israel

Appendix-2

15th July, 1936.

H. Kallenbach, Esq.,
South African Zionist Federation,
P.O. Box 18,
Johannesburg, South Africa.

Dear Dr. Kallenbach,

I am addressing myself to you without having the privilege of knowing you personally but I have heard about you from many friends on account of your Zionist activities, and more particularly, of your Indian associations.

It is the subject of India that causes me to write to you. The problem of establishing contacts with the Indian world and of gaining sympathy and understanding for our work and aspirations among leaders of the Indian renaissance has long occupied our attention. It is clear that our political future as of a nation returning to its home in Asia must ultimately depend in a large measure on the amount of good-will and solidarity which we shall succeed in evolving on the part of the great Asiatic civilisations. Even from the purely materialistic standpoint a country like India with its vast potentialities holds out to us prospects of marketing and other economic advantages which we cannot overlook, and we must see to it that if ever these prospects begin to materialise they should not be hampered by political or racial prejudice.

In the course of recent years we had a number of opportunities to welcome to Palestine guests from India of varying degrees of prominence who had made a special point of visiting the country on their way to or from Europe. They all displayed a very keen and genuine interest in our work and carried away with them definitely favourable impressions. Some of them suggested to us the advisibility, from our point of view, of sending people to India in order to acquaint the intelligentzia of the Indian national movement with Zionist aims and achievements. They seemed to believe that in Hindu circles such efforts on our part would find a favourable response.

The present disturbances and the widespread interest in the political controversy raging in Palestine which they have aroused in the countries of both East and West appear to us to have brought this problem to a head. I know that the Palestine events are widely discussed in the Indian press and political circles. I myself have received a couple of letters from men who have been here on a visit enquiring what it is all about. I do not know whether you follow the Indian press or correspond with your friends there to the extent of knowing exactly what is the general Indian reaction to the occurrences here. I regret to have to state that it is on the whole unfavourable to us.

Needless to say, I am referring to the Hindu community and not to the Mohammedans, the hostility of many of whom to the Jewish effort in Palestine is well known. The Indian National Congress is reported to have identified itself with the Khilafat circles in its attitude on the Palestine problem. A man like Nehru is said to have openly taken up a stand against us. The general tendency among Hindu politicians appears to be to regard us Jews in Palestine as intruders coming from the west. Once the conflict between us and the Arabs is conceived as one between Asiatics and westerners, or westernisers, it becomes a matter of instinct—not even of political reasoning—for the Hindus to side against the Jews.

The question of making a beginning with the presentation of our case in India is thus becoming a matter of urgency. It will clearly be much more difficult to fight misconceptions after they have hardened and gained currency than to prevent their formation. We have accordingly decided to take action at once and have proposed to Dr. Immanuel Olsvanger, whom you know well, to go to India for two or three months' stay, to be the first Zionist emissary who would bring our message, personally and directly, to the leaders of modern India. What we have in mind is not any form of political campaign to be conducted by means of public meetings, interviews in the press etc., but a very cautious and discreet method of procedure—mainly individual talks with people that matter, possibly addresses to small and closed circles of interested persons. If Dr. Olsvanger is able to establish good personal contacts with a couple of dozen Indian leaders of the intellectual type and to get a hearing for our case in the most important political and intellectual centres—so that some basis is created upon which we might continue to build in the future—I would consider his mission a success. I would add that Dr. Olsvanger is a candidate of my own choosing. I have known him for years and I have faith not only in his ability to place the presentation of the Zionist case on a high cultural level, but to earn the respect and affection of persons with whom he comes into contact. To my mind, and judging by his experience with some Arab people here, he is particularly gifted to gain the confidence and even endear himself to persons with an oriental mentality. Moreover, he knows a great deal about the world of Indian culture and has a few but important personal connections in India. From all possible candidates whom we have at our disposal here he is decidedly the best. But even endowed as he is, he will be embarking on a very risky adventure in tackling this difficult proposition alone, in having to rely on other people's introductions and to grope about until he will find the right people to talk to and the right way to approach them. We had thought of asking you to introduce Olsvanger to your friends in India, but on giving the matter further consideration and upon the advice of some of our South African friends here I have decided to approach you with a more far-reaching request.

It is that you yourself should go to India to take part in, or rather to lead, this mission. I realise how startling it must appear to a man in your position to be so suddenly faced with a proposal of breaking his ordinary business routine to go off to a distant country on an errand of which he may never have dreamt. But our movement is passing through dangerous times—its whole future is now at stake—and one really feels justified in these circumstances to call upon others to make unusual sacrifices. South African Zionism as a whole and every one of its leaders individually have behind them a splendid record of Zionist service in terms of internal unity, discipline, devotion and financial exertion. But all these are ordinary ways of serving Zion. There are but few people whom circumstances have placed in a position enabling them to render service of an extraordinary character. I am advised and believe that you are at the present moment such a person. The fact that there are Indians in South Africa and that there are Jews there who at a certain time identified themselves so closely with the Indian cause was, historically speaking, a mere accident. But circumstances arise when such historical accidents assume deep import and may truly be regarded as the work of Providence. Be that as it may, the fact remains that by virtue of your signal service to the Indian cause in South Africa and your close personal connection with the greatest of living Hindus—a connection which I know has its ramifications—you are in a unique position to help Zionism in a field where the resources of the Jewish people are so meagre as to be practically non-existent. What you have no doubt regarded as a part of your purely private past which has nothing to do with Zionist or Jewish affairs can now be of invaluable service to our national movement—it can, so to speak, be "nationalised", and with eminently useful effect. I hope that you will not withhold this service, in regard to which you stand unrivalled among Zionists, from our common cause.

I should be grateful if you would kindly inform me of your decision by cable as soon as you possibly can manage after the receipt of this letter, for 'Olsvanger is getting ready for the journey and he will not start before we have heard from you. It would be better if you did not mention anything about India in your cable but referred generally to the proposed trip. If your cable calls for a reply on my part I shall probably arrange for the cable to be sent to you from Cairo as it is preferable that this proposal should not receive publicity in Palestine at present.

I am taking the liberty of sending a copy of this letter to Mr. N. Kirschner of Benoni for his confidential information.

Yours very sincerely

M. Shertok

CZA S25/3239

P.O. Box 2493,
Johannesburg.
25th July, 1936.

Dear Mr. Shertok,

I thank you for your letter of the 15th instant. The contents have not come quite as a surprise, as with Mr. Braudo and Dr. Weizman, discussions on similar lines have taken place.

Your letter arrived, when I was just preparing to leave for London. I have not been following up matters in India during many years, and did not know how India has reacted on present day occurrences in Palestine. I have only read "Young India" during its publication, and now "Harijan". The latter, as you know, is not a political paper. It has been news to me that some Hindu leaders are favouring the political aspirations of certain Arab people. Doubtless the position justifies your anxiety and your action.

Our people are going through most anxious times and none of us should refuse the call for service, when it arrives. I am coming. I am a man of ordinary intelligence, past 65 years, having devoted the last 22 years almost entirely to technical-commercial pursuits. My services will at best be limited.

Dr. O. should be the right choice for this mission. I know him well and his keen interest for Eastern people and customs. I shall do what I can, and am looking forward to join him in Palestine, or elsewhere. Dr. O. is not to wait for me if his early departure is decided upon.

Mr. K. has cabled you—"Party sailing for England next week can be in Palestine early October prepared undertake trip cable whether time suits your plan" and we expect to hear from you.

I am leaving Cape Town for London on Friday the 31st July, 1936. My London address is care of the Standard Bank Limited, 10, Clements Lane, Lombard Street, London E.C. and the cable address is Kallenbach care Africorum, London. When in London I shall remain in communication with Professor Brodetzky.

With kind regards, to you and Dr. O.

Yours very sincerely

H. Kallenbach-

CZA S25/3239

C/o Mahatma Gandhi
Tithal, Bulsar, (B.B. & C.I.)
1. VI. 1937

My dear Mr. Shertok,

I trust my two telegrams from Port Said have reached you. I desire to thank you and Mrs. Shertok again for the very kind interest, you have taken in me and the guidance, you have afforded me during my stay in Palestine. The days I spent there are not to be forgotten.

The voyage on the "Maloja" which I had to board on the 12th May at 7 a.m. passed quickly, the weather was quite bearable and we reached Bombay, as intended, on the 20th May. I was received there by Mahatma Gandhi's third son, Ramdas, and some of his friends. I had all assistance, I could wish for, on landing on this vast, strange and so exceptional interesting country. A personal note of welcome from M.G. asked me to proceed by the first available train, if not otherwise engaged, to his present abode, where he with some close associates is taking a "so-called" rest at a friend's house for a few weeks. The afternoon of the 20th May was used to view Bombay, this huge port-city of $1\frac{1}{4}$ million people. My Bombay hosts succeeded in giving me a good idea of its lay-out, the town is built on seven islands. I entrained the same night, accompanied by Ramdas Gandhi, to Tithal, a colony of large substantial houses with fine palm-gardens, situated practically at the shore of the Indian Ocean, four hours by train north of Bombay. We arrived at Tithal at about 4.30 a.m. when M.G. with a small band of friends and disciples were holding morning prayers. It was still dark. We squatted quietly and silently on the floor. The prayers completed, I received a very hearty welcome from M.G. I felt and still feel—the 23 years of separation non-existent. Just as in South Africa we eat together and sleep next to each other. It is a different world to the West, with which the great part of our people and we, I feel sorry to say, have so fully associated themselves. Perhaps this is one of the reasons, why we have not been able so far to overcome some of our difficulties in Palestine, with its eastern habits and culture.

There is here, and what I have been able to observe elsewhere, much simplicity, the people are natural and so humanized that one cannot but wholeheartedly associate himself with them. I feel at home here.

With exception of two days, which I spent at Bardoli and its neighbourhood to see some village life—there are 700,000 villages in India—and at Haripura, the place chosen for the National Congress, to be held February next, where at the big river Tapti, 100,000 people and more will congregate daily for eight days, I have been and am staying with M.G.

There are great and urgent problems in front of M.G. and this band of unselfish and untiring workers, concerning the fate of many millions of people. Notwithstanding this M.G. has an open heart and a ready ear for all comers who pour their troubles, hopes and joys into this receptive and so understanding soul and so he also listens patiently to me.

M.G. has various pamphlets, you provided me with. The statements, you intended to furnish me with, have not reached me, I shall be glad to have same. I have had various discussions with M.G. and others on Palestine matters about which I shall write to you again.

Our timetable here is as follows:

To rise	4.00 a.m.
Morning Prayer	4.20 "
Walk at sea-shore	5.30 "
I. meal	10.30 "
II. meal	5.30 p.m.
Walk at sea-shore	6.30 " ⎫ participated by many
Evening prayer	7.30 " ⎬ people outside the
To retire, on hard beds,	household
blankets or floor in the open	9.30 "

M.G. and the members of the household are spinning daily for some time which is often carried on whilst dictating letters, during discussions, interviews and meetings. With kindest regards to you and Mrs. Shertok.

Yours very sincerely

H. K.

P.S. Kindly instruct your Secretary to send copies each of a good history book of Jews and Rev. I.H. Holmes book on Palestine to M.G.'s associate and secretary: Mahadev Desai Esq. Maganwadi, Wardha, C.P. India, and to the leader of the Congress party in Madras C. Rajagopalachari Esq. 49 Bazlullah Road, P.O. Thyagarajnagar, Madras, India and also to each a set of the pamphlets, you gave me for M.G.

To the first address one or two boxes of grape fruit or other citrus fruit as a trial order (marked "Perishable"), if there is any hope that the contents of the boxes arrive here in sound condition. The costs for books and fruit to be charged to me. The account to be sent to Mr. Gering (Mr. Braudo's associate) or to me P.O. Box 2493, Johannesburg. The books forwarded to Anna Lewin and Mr. and Mrs. Braudo c/o The Agency please forward. Kindly let me have Anna Lewin's address and also 3-4 sets of the pamphlets and copies of statement still outstanding.

Please reply to: Maganwadi, Wardha C.P. India.

Appendix-3

What Mrs. Sarojini Naidu said to the Bene-Israels in 1916

Under the auspices of the Bene-Israel Mitra Mandal, Mrs. Sarojini Naidu, the well-known poetess of India, delivered an eloquent and stirring address in her usual sweet and sonorous voice, on Sunday the 16th January 1916 at 10 A.M. in the Noorbaug Hall. Miss Rebecca Reuben, B.A., presided. With the exception of a few non-Jew guests, the spacious hall was packed to overcrowding by Bene-Israel ladies and gentlemen.

The gifted *devi* depicted in most flattering and touching terms the past glory of Israel exhibiting both her close study and deep sympathy. Her pictures of the great lawgiver, noble prophets and sweet-singers in Israel were vivid and admirable. With vigour she referred to the distinguished role played by Israel in the realms of Art and Literature, Politics and Finance. Dealing with the transcendentalism of Spinoza and the melodies

of that crippled Jew, Heine, she combined the truth of history
with the deepest pathos of poetry. Without fear of exaggeration
we unhesitatingly declare that it was an exquisite address, and a
treat, rare and unique. While on the main topic, she pointed out
that although the Jews were widely divided from their native
land, they still remained Jews; however remote from each other,
they were still brethren. These singular people held together
under most adverse circumstances, and their example is
unparalleled in History. The principle characteristics which kept
the flame of their religion steady and their nationality
unextinguishable, she said, were three. The Jews were law
abiding, the Jews were pure and the Jews were proud of their
race. Their law was irreversible and the perpetuity whereof they
were steadfastly convinced and to which they adhered
pertinaciously. That very law taught them scrupulous purity of
person, mind and spirit, and that law instilled in them the idea of
their being God's First-born, His Priests and His Soldiers. They
therefore felt proud of their position, and of their race. Endowed
with these characteristics the Jews in India should, in addition to
their own communal development, contribute their share in the
building up of Indian Nationality and in heralding the era of
peace and prosperity to the *Bharatwarsh*, a singular land, which
alone welcomed them with open arms and freely allowed them
to dwell amongst its children without causing any loss of human
blood.

Miss Reuben rose equal to the high occasion. Her summing
up and exhortations gave full indications that before long she
would occupy a prominent place amongst the distinguished
personages in Israel and in India.

Mr. Aptekar was in charge of the thanksgiving, the ring of sincerity of which removed it from the usual conventional plane.

The audience dispersed highly pleased and in full admiration for the high attainments of Mrs. Naidu.

The Bene-Israel Mitra Mandal thus came to light for the first time and has made a very happy beginning. We welcome all high-minded efforts conducive to the uplift of our community. We heartily congratulate the Mandal for its first success and offer our thanks for the intellectual treat they provided for us by inducing Mrs. Naidu to spare an hour amidst her multifarious engagements during her recent visit to Bombay to deliver an instructive and inspiring address to our community. We wish the Mandal a long, active and useful life and success in its disinterested undertakings.

reproduced from *India & Israel, Oct. 1951, Vol. IV, No. 4.*

Dr. Immanuel Olsvanger
Jerusalem

Bombay 13.10.36.
The Ritz Hotel

Mrs. Sarojini Naidu
Hiderabad

Dear Mrs. Naidu,

On my return to Bombay I was very sorry to hear of your illness. I once saw a painting of some famous physician sitting at his desk. On the desk there was a candle burnt to the half. And underneath it the inscription "Aliis inserviendo consumor". That is a beautiful motto for all public servants And I had ample occasion to see how you made this motto your own in the grand service you render to your people and to all that is human. But you must take care of yourself. You must regain complete health and strength. You are needed in all your vigour, love and humour for many many decades more.

When you are completely recovered, do take a short holiday and come on a pleasure trip to Palestine. I will see to that both Jews and Arabs receive you with honour and affection.

Only to-day I read your speech on the 28-th of September in Bombay ("Palestine day"). I thank you for that speech. I quite understand that it required much courage from you to speak thus at that meeting. It is the more beautiful. When you are in Palestine, you will convince yourself that the grand work done by the Jews in Palestine really deserves a word of greetings from outside. One day the world will see how the two sections of the two great and ancient civilisations, Jewish and Arab, live in peaceful and brotherly cooperation in Palestine. You might be interested to know, that in reply to a letter I addressed on the Palestine question to Khan Abdulghaffar Khan, he said amongst others"...... it would be a great gain to humanity if both the parties (meaning Jews and Arabs. I. Olsv.) could come to an amicable understanding without the interference of an outside authority."

When in Madras, I stayed at a hotel and saw on the visitors list a name Miss L. Naidu. Being sure that it was your daughter whom I met here I sent in my card. But the lady replied that she does not know me. So, evidently it was a mistake. If that lady is one of your family and should you meet her, please explain to her the misunderstanding and transmit to her my apologies.

Please don't take the trouble to reply to this letter if it is too strenuous for you, but a few lines from you will be greatly appreciated by me. Yourself and your daughter were really so very kind and helpful to me, that I feel your absence now very much.

With highest esteem and most cordial greetings.

Yours affectionately

C.F. Andrews, the Gentile Zionist

A less illuminated side of C.F. Andrews was his sympathy with Jews; his support of Zionism; and his efforts to find asylum in India for Jews fleeing the Holocaust. There was no, reason why this side should have lain in darkness as his biographers[1] had access to his papers at Vishva-Bharati at Santiniketan in West Bengal and these papers do cover all these aspects. There is a letter, for example, from his Jewish friend in South Africa, Hermann Kallenbach, an ardent Zionist:

> My people require helpers like you. Millions of us go under now under German rule in Austria, Czechoslovakia and Poland, but every man saved may be a potential helper to his people.[2]

While he was alive, Andrews did not conceal his sympathy with the Jews. On January 8, 1932, he gave a long, exclusive, interview to the "South African Jewish Chronicle" in which he clearly stated his opinions. It is worth quoting extracts from this interview. Andrews started by saying the following:

> I have every sympathy with the Jews in their wish to go back to Palestine which is their fatherland and must always remain their fatherland, and I cannot possibly imagine that the difficulties of making it once more their spiritual and temporal home are insuperable.

He added that all through his life he had some of his greatest friends among Jews in almost every country:

---

1. Benarsidas Chaturvedi and Marjorie Sykes: *Charles Freer Andrews* (Harper, NY, 1950) and P.C. Roy Chaudhury: *C.F. Andrews* (Somaiya Publications, Bombay, 1971). In Chaturvedi & Sykes there are refs. to Palestine on pp. 300, 303, 312–315.
2. Kallenbach to Andrews, Johannesburg, 3.1.1940. Andrews also published an article called "Persecuted Humanity in Central Europe—The Curse of Anti-Semitism".

> I don't think that this is unexpected, because ever since I began to think seriously, I have been a humanitarian and an internationalist, and have found that the best of friends and workers in any international cause, which I have undertaken at different times have been the Jews. For instance, here in South Africa, when I first came out to help Mr. Ghandhi (sic) in his great passive resistance struggle on behalf of the indentured Indian labourers, almost every one who helped me directly (apart from the Indians themselves) was either a man or woman belonging to the Jewish community. Far more of my fellow-workers were Jews than men belonging to my own religion.

It had exactly been the same in New York, Australia, and in other parts of the world, he explained. For this reason he had shared very deeply the sorrow which the Jewish community as a whole felt about the position of Palestine.

As this interview was given a year before Hitler came to power in Germany, there is no mention, obviously, of Jewish refugees. His role in this matter was acknowledged eight years later when he died. Another Jewish friend of Gandhi, Henry S.L. Polak, wrote in a letter to the London "Jewish Chronicle" that Andrews had

> a deep and abiding love for the Jewish people and a warm sympathy for them in the tragic happenings that have befallen them in recent years in so many parts of the world. He had several intimate Jewish friends, and until his last illness I had been in the habit of sending him material drawn from your columns and those of other Jewish papers relating to the sorrows of Jewry. One of the things he had made especially his own during his last stay in India was to explain the Jewish point of view to his Indian friends through the Press and otherwise, and to seek help for Jewish refugees so that some of them might find a home and suitable work in India. His death is a real blow to Jewry.[3]

---

3. Reprinted in "The Jewish Tribune", May, 1940.

One such message was sent by Andrews from Santiniketan on February 18, 1939, and appeared in all the leading Indian newspapers:

> What is needed is to discover by what practical steps India as a whole can take her part along with other nations in the humanitarian refugee work.

The message continued:

> The question of relief for the Jews who were been driven out by the Nazi regime in Central Europe had been absorbing for some months past my closest attention and I hope in the near future to be able to take part in a public meeting in Calcutta summoned for that purpose. At Santiniketan we have already done something to help in this cause and hope to be able to do more. But a nationwide effort is needed. At a time when scientific problems are facing India in all directions, the opportunity should not be lost of gaining the help of some of the finest scientists in the world, who are of Jewish origin. Above all heartfelt sympathy is needed combined with practical aid. Some of my dearest and truest friends have been Jews; and I know the same could be said of Mahatma Gandhi. When I went out to South Africa for the first time in 1913 to help the Indian cause the three noblest supporters of that cause belonged to the Hebrew race. Two had suffered imprisonment and one had been chosen by Mahatma Gandhi to carry on the work at the centre which he had been obliged to leave undone when he courted imprisonment.

Alas, Andrews' role finding asylum in India for Jewish refugees is conspicuous by its absence in the otherwise excellent book, *Jewish Exile In India* (1933–1945).[4] True the editors of the book and Andrews' biographers had no access to the Kallenbach papers. These papers are still held by the family in Haifa, Israel.

---

4. Edited by Anil Bhatti and Johannes H. Voigt (Manohar, Delhi, 1999).

The original letters of Gandhi to Kallenbach were bought by the Indian Government and these are lodged in the National Archives in New Delhi. There are forty-three letters, including two telegrams, from Andrews to Kallenbach, most handwritten and some typed. Inspite of having these letters, the book published privately by the family does not make full use of them.[5] This paper is based mainly on these letters.

Andrews had a commission from the English publishers, Allen and Unwin, to write a book on the life of Christ. In order to do this properly, he felt he needed to visit Palestine. While there he intended to see first hand the political situation and decide how he could help. By 1933 he had made contact with the Zionist leaders including Chaim Weizmann who later became Israel's first President. Weizmann encouraged such a visit:

> I know the Rev. C.F. Andrews very well, and have had many a talk with him about Palestine. I believe it might be of great use to have him visit the country. He is tactful and carries much weight in Moslem circles. I believe the matter was discussed at some length while I was in South Africa, and we agreed that we should do anything we could to encourage Mr. Andrews' visit to Palestine.[6]

Weizmann even invited him to stay with him in Jerusalem. Hermann Kallenbach too was supportive and gave Andrews 200 pounds sterling for the trip. Andrews was grateful for the money as he preferred to receive financial help from neutral sources. He insisted on going out "as a private individual doing my own works in my own way and writing my book on Christ while at the same time acting in every way I could as a peace maker and lover of mankind. I know that Dr. Weizmann would fully agree

---

5. Isa Sarid and Christian Bartolf: *Hermann Kallenbach, Mahatma Gandhi's Friend in South Africa.* Besides the 43 letters, there are 16 other letters and telegrams from Andrews to Kallenbach's niece, Hanna Lazar. Hanna visited Gandhi in India. Copies of some of Andrews' letters to Kallenbach are now lodged in the archives at Santiniketan.

6. Weizmann to Morris Kentridge, London, 4 August 1933, in *The Letters and Papers of Chaim Weizmann* (Gen. Ed. Barnet Litvinoff, Jerusalem, 1978), Vol. XVI, pp. 15 & 16. Andrews also met David Ben-Gurion. See Ben-Gurion's *Diary,* entry dated 16.6.1937.

with this for he is an exceedingly good man. The other whom I have learnt greatly to revere and trust through what he has written is Dr. Magnes. I have a very deep longing to meet him. He has some of the qualities of the old Hebrew prophets and understands their spirit".[7] Andrews' own ideal for the Jewish people was

> that they should be the link between East and West, and should be able to keep the peace between them, but in order to do this they must themselves become "Sons of Peace".[8]

However Andrews was not uncritical of the Zionist leadership:

> Sometimes, when I have read Mr. Sokolow's speeches, I have been little afraid that his whole heart is not bent towards peace but conquest. I am telling you some of my fears rather than giving you any facts on which they are based for it is rather an instinct as I read what he says than a definite disagreement with his actual words.[9]

Andrews read everything that he could find on the whole Jewish Question:

> There is *(i)* a very interesting work, rather critical of Zionism, by Israel Zangwill called "The Voice of Jerusalem", then there is *(ii)* "The Old Testament and After" by a very noble Liberal Jew, Claude Montefiore and *(iii)* "Zionism and Judaism" by Achad Ha-am. These three noble books hold different views.[10]

---

7. Andrews to Kallenbach, April 21, 1937. In another to Kallenbach dated April 16, 1937, Andrews makes it clear that he would not take any money from any Association "which might render my work of peace-making more difficult and precarious". In the end Andrews did not use the money and Kallenbach requested that the money be passed on to Andrews' sisters (K. to Henry Polak, 12.5.1940).
8. Andrews to Kallenbach, Durban, 2nd. August, 1934.
9. Ibid.
10. Andrews to Kallenbach, Santiniketan, Jan. 26, 1938.

Gandhi approved of the visit but advised Andrews that he write the book in India and revise it in Palestine. In 1937, in two letters[11] to Rabindranath Tagore, Andrews put forward his plans:

> I have had a commission to write a life of Christ in which the Eastern side will not be left out as so often has happened in the past. This 'Life of Christ' (it must obviously be the very best that I can do) will need a visit to Palestine at *some* (sic) time, before it is finished, but Mahatmaji said to me yesterday the he had felt at once (when I wrote to him about the commission) that Palestine would *not* (sic) be the place in which to *write* (sic) it but rather the place in which to *revise* (sic) it when I *had* (sic) written it; and that I should write it in this country (India) and make it such that those among whom my life had been spent in the East should confirm it as true to their own Eastern tradition: for that is the object of this new 'Life of Christ'. Mahatmaji is quite clear that I should write the outline, at least in India rather than in Palestine.

At about the same time he wrote to Kallenbach[12] explaining why he wanted to stay in India a little longer before going to Palestine. He agreed with Gandhi as "Bapu has practical wisdom which carries me with it". He felt "the time for me has not yet come" as the British partition proposal for Palestine" is being held in suspense" and a "third party cannot come in at a time like that". The final reason (the second in the letter) is worth quoting in full:

> My presence here (in India) in relation to this whole question is of great importance. I was *not* (sic) satisfied

---

11. Andrews to Gurudev, Wardha, Aug. 9 (no year given; probably 1937); and 13.8.1937. In a letter to Agatha Harrison dated Feb. 17, 1939, Andrews writes that "Mahatmaji with his amazing insight into my own character told me that I must write the book in India and I feel that this is true. England would throw me off my balance and possibly make the book an 'English book' which would not be of much help to any one. As what is needed is rather to fill up the picture where the West has failed to draw the right lines".
12. Andrews to Kallenbach, Wardha, Aug. 11, 1937.

with Bapu's own statement.[13] It seemed to me too abstract. At the same time I liked the main idea that the Jews ought to *win* (sic) the Arabs, not use an interested power from outside to coerce them. But there were many qualifications which immediately occurred to me and I should like to talk out that whole position with Dr. Magnes whom I trust wholeheartedly even though I have never met him. I am thinking on the same lines as Bapu, namely, that as both sides are unhappy at this thought of Partition there may be an opening for an agreed settlement in which force will not enter. That is my thought as well as Bapu's but to *explain* (sic) this is too long for a letter; yet at least you will easily see that by gathering the thought trends here, in India, I may do more to make clear the true Jewish position with which I have such deep sympathy here in India and this may be better than going at once to Palestine. Here, in an extraordinary way, is the key to the whole question; and when I am near to Bapu I feel I almost have it in my hand, even though I am unsatisfied with his present position. I regard it as an imperfect one, not as an untrue one. I am sure you will understand the distinction.

If Andrews finished his book, he would have gone to Palestine. In his mind the two issues were linked. There were, however, serious interruptions in his writing not least his advancing years and deteriorating health. But, perhaps, it was the Holocaust that eventually put paid to his "Life of Christ" and his dream of visiting the Holy Land. A letter to Kallenbach in 1939 illustrates how busy he was with Jewish refugee rehabilitation:

I have been very busily occupied with the German Refugee Jews who are in India and have been

---

13. In July, 1937, Gandhi made his final statement on Zionism and gave it to Kallenbach. This statement is in the Central Zionist Archives at Jerusalem, S25 3587. Gandhi's main point was that the "Jews should disclaim any intention of realising their aspiration under the protection of arms (or the British) and should rely wholly on the goodwill of Arabs".

interned. My position and standing with the Congress and with the Government also makes it possible for me to render help in the most deserving cases. I enclose Dr. Aronson's letters whom I was able to get taken into Santiniketan and who was interned and then released. I am in close touch with the Bombay Relief Assn. and also the Calcutta Branch. The most important cases nearly always come to me and I have been able to get some of them posted in positions where at least they may earn something. Sir Ismail Mirza of Mysore has been good and others also.[14]

The British Indian Government in Delhi demanded that an immigrant had to be politically acceptable and have a guarantee from a person living in India so that he or she would never be a financial liability to the State. Until this was done, the immigrant was placed in a detention centre as an enemy alien. So there were instances when a Jew was detained together with a diehard Nazi! Andrews, as an Englishman, used his political clout in Delhi to ease the rules so that more immigrants could enter the country and those detained released. Parallel with this he worked with the Jewish communities in India as they could take the practical steps to help their European brethren. At the end of 1938 a committee was formed under the aegis of Sir Victor Sassoon to find suitable workplaces and guarantee eventual return journeys. The Jewish Relief Organisation in Bombay and Calcutta helped the immigrants financially and psychologically. However, Andrews' work did not stop there. He wanted to inform Indian public opinion on the Holocaust. This meant using his influence with the media and at the meetings of the Congress Party. He pointed out to Kallenbach that "I am doing far more by remaining here to forward the cause of the persecuted Jews than I could possibly do by going to Palestine itself".[15] He continued:

I have been trying in every way to stop the agitation here against the Jews and have succeeded so far better

---

14. Andrews to Kallenbach, Santiniketan, Nov. 27, 1939. See also Ezra Yehezkel-Shaked: *The Jews Opium and The Kimono* (Rubin Mass, Jerusalem) Chapter 9, "India, the quiet station at the crossroads".
15. Andrews to Kallenbach, The Ashram, Tirupattur, Sept. 20, 1938.

than I could have expected. There can be no doubt at all that the attitude has changed and that if I had not remained here in India corresponding with leading Congress people and pointing out the cruelty of upholding alongwith Germany and other countries an Anti-Semitic policy things might have been incredibly worse.

He did his utmost to spread through the Press the most reliable account of the persecution of the Jews. He praised Gandhi's son, Devadas, then editor of the "Hindustan Times", "who has taken what I have sent him".[16] His success with Congress was, however, mixed:

My whole heart is in the attempt in this country to condemn the Nazi Cruelty openly and effectively. I tried hard to get a full clause put into a Congress resolution and though in part it was done it was rather overshadowed by the upholding of the Arab cause as if there was nothing to be said for the Zionist position. What I am now hoping to do is to get both from the poet and Subash Bose the strongest possible condemnation of the Nazi persecution.[17]

Andrews succeeded with Tagore but not with Bose.[18]

---

16. Andrews to Kallenbach, Bangalore, August 31, 1938.
17. A. to K., Santiniketan, 14/3/1939. See P.R. Kumaraswamy: "India and the Holocaust: Perceptions of the Indian National Congress (Journal of Indo-Judaic Studies, April, 2000). The Resolution read: "While sympathizing with the plight of Jews in Europe and elsewhere, the Committee deplores that in Palestine the Jews have relied on British armed forces to advance their special claims and thus aligned themselves on the side of British imperialism."
18. Leonard A Gordon in "Bengal: The Nationalist Movement 1876-1940" (New York 1974) maintains that S.C. Bose was not really anti-semitic. He wrote and said things against Jews without really believing them. He was mainly concerned with getting rid of the British even if it meant going to the devil. The enemy of my enemy is my friend. See also *The Indian Express*, March 3, 2002 (the Express Magazine, Section III, p. 1.). Dr. Walter Norden, the veteran journalist, recalls the conversations he had with Bose in a German U-Boat going from Norway to Madagascar at the height of World War II (Norden was then an eighteen year old torpedo engineer): "Bose was less impressed by Hitler of whom he spoke only once. Hitler too, for his part, was equally unable to make sense of Bose as a personage. Hitler is on record of having commented: 'These Indians because of their religious beliefs are incapable of killing even a fly. How do they expect to win a war' ".

THE JEWS OF INDIA

Written in conjunction with Mr. Isaac Sankar, a genealogist, living in Eilat, Israel, who has done fieldwork in India and is fluent in Hindi and Marathi and can read the Modi script. Mr. Sankar and the author are working on the Bene Israel Jews under the Marathas from Shivaji to 1818.

The Jews of India with Special Reference to the Bene Israel

When dealing with Jews one must realise that one is dealing with very small numbers. The world Jewish population today stands at just fourteen million. At most the Jews in India numbered about 30,000. They formed only 0.01% of the Indian population—hardly a drop in the ocean. The majority of these Jews (well over 60%) were the Bene Israel or the Children of Israel. Before looking in detail at this community, here is a brief round up of the other Jewish communities in India.

Chronologically the Jews who settled in Kerala could be the oldest Jewish community in India, that is, if the Ophir mentioned in the Bible was in India. One reads in the so-called "Old Testament"[1] that King Solomon, who reigned in Israel in the tenth century B.C.E,[2] sent ships to Ophir and that these ships brought back monkeys, peacocks, elephants, sandalwood, and gold.[3] If Ophir was in India (and there is strong evidence, particularly linguistic, that it was), then it was probably somewhere in Kerala.

The historians of the Syrian Christians of Kerala have no doubt that Ophir was in India. They maintain that the Jewish settlements in Kerala paved the way for St. Thomas, the disciple of Jesus, who they claim founded their Church and who they believe came to India in 52 C.E.[4] What is interesting is that the seven Churches that they believe were founded by St Thomas were (except probably for one) near Jewish settlements[5]. What, however, is beyond dispute is that the Jews came to Kerala some

---

1. The Jews call it the "Tanak".
2. *Before the Common or Christian Era* (B.C.).
3. See I Kings 9:28 in "Tanak".
4. Common or Christian Era (A.D.). See *The St. Thomas Christian Encyclopaedia of India* edited by George Manachery, 1982, 2 vols.
5. Cranganore, Parur, Palayur, Quilon, Kokamanglam (near Jewish settloment of Muttom), Nivanam (near Quilon), and Chayal. Chayal was not near a Jewish settlement but as it was a marketing centre there may well have been Jews there. Marco Polo (1293) speaks of Jews at Quilon.

years before or after the destruction of the second Temple in Jerusalem by the Romans in 70 C.E.

The Jews of Cochin have copper plates which they date as 379 C.E.[6] The writing on the Plates reads in translation that Sri Parkaran Iravi Vanmar granted to Joseph Rabban the village of Anjuvannam. As it also states that he was entitled to a palanquin and parasol, he apparently had the status of a king. The scrolls close with these words:

> To Joseph Rabban, the Prince of Anjuvannam, and to his descendants, sons and daughters, and to his nephews, and to sons-in-law who married his daughters in natural succession, so long as the world and moon exist, Anjuvannam shall be his hereditary possession.

Anjuvannam is identified as being the ancient port of Cranganore or Shingly. This means that for centuries the Jews in Cranganore had virtually an independent principality. A fourteenth century Hebrew poet and traveller, Rabbi Nissim, wrote:

> I travelled from Spain,
> I had heard of the city of Shingly,
> I longed to see an Israel king,
> Him, I saw with my own eyes.

The Portuguese put an end to this kingdom in 1565. The Jews fled to neighbouring Cochin and received the protection of the Maharajah. For the next four hundred years the Jews are treated with a liberality that surpasses all understanding. Here it should be emphasised that the Jewish experience in India was unique in Jewish history in that there was no antisemitism whatsoever. The Jews were not discriminated against, expelled or exterminated, something that had been their common lot elsewhere. The Jews, for example, were expelled from England in 1290. In 1655, under Cromwell, they trickled back into England. One weighty argument used by the Dutch Rabbi, Menasseh ben Israel, in his successful petition to Cromwell was a reference to the happiness

---

6. This date has been contested. Another possibility is that the copper plates were granted by Raja Bhaskar Ravi Varmar I (962–1020).

and tolerance enjoyed by the Jews of Cochin under a Hindu ruler. So one can say without exaggeration that the Maharajah of Cochin, a Nair, shamed England into taking back the Jews! Sad to relate that there are just 16 Jews left in Jew Town in Cochin at the time of writing. The over four hundred year old synagogue—the oldest in the Commonwealth—is now a national, historic monument open to the public.

Probably the best known Jewish community in India was the Iraqi one mainly due to the fame of the Sassoon family often referred to as the Rothschilds of the East. There was a saying in Iraq: "If you get to India, you will get rich".[7] However, this Iraqi or Baghdadi community did include Jews from other Muslim countries like Persia, Syria, Afganistan and the Yemen. It is known that Surat had Jews living there in 1664 when Shivaji raided the town.[8] By 1797, there were about 95 Jews, mainly merchants from the Middle East, in Surat.[9] One of these Jews left Surat in 1798 for Bengal and is considered the first Jew of Calcutta.[10] With the decline of Surat, the remaining Jews left en masse for Mumbai.

The real influx of Iraqi Jews into India came during the 1820s. These Jews were fleeing the draconian laws passed by the Ottomans who then controlled Iraq. One of these laws was forced conscription into the Ottoman army. It was in this wave it immigration that the founder of the Sassoon family came to India. However, in his case, he fled as his family had lost favour with the Sultan.[11]

---

7. "Thus thou seest the masses of this country labour under the impression that whoever goes to India becomes rich". These were the exact words of the Jewish sage, Sa'adia Gaon (882–942), who lived in Iraq.
8. See "Shivaji's Raid Upon Surat in 1664" by William Foster in "The Indian Antiquary", December 1921, p. 314.
9. Surat still has an ancient cemetery to attest to the Jewish presence there.
10. He was Shalom Aharon Ovadiah Hacohen who originally came from Aleppo in Syria. One should hurriedly point out that there were Jews in Calcutta before 1798. They came with the British East India Company but were temporary residents. When one talks about a permanent Jewish settlement one assumes that there would at least be a synagogue and a cemetery.
11. Heskell Gabbai, a minister at Istanbul, Turkey, and his brother, Ezra, were murdered. Sassoon, who was in jail with Ezra, managed to escape. There are now less than hundred Iraqi Jews living in Calcutta. There are a few hundred Iraqi Jews left in Mumbai and only three in Pune. See Dalia Ray. "The Jewish Heritage of Calcutta" (Minerva, Kolkata, 2001)

For a long time it was believed that just three Jewish communities resided in India: The Bene Israel; the Cochini; and the Iraqi. However, thanks to a recent book published by Manohar and edited by Prof. Anil Bhatti and Johannes H. Voight, it is now established that there was a fourth. The book entitled, *Jewish Exile In India* (1933–1945), deals with the one thousand or so European Jews who fled the Holocaust and found asylum in India.

One cannot conclude this brief survey of Indian Jews without mentioning the "Benei Menashe of Manipur". There were Jews living in China for centuries in the ancient capital of Kai Feng Fu. These Jews disappeared during the nineteenth century. The Benei Menashe claim they are descendants of Chinese Jews. They surfaced in North East India twenty five years ago. Research on them is still in its infancy.

After this brief survey, it is time to return to the Bene Israel. They arrived in India in at least 175 B.C.E. They were shipwrecked off the coast of Konkan. Those who survived swam ashore and found themselves in the village of Novgaon. Their first act was to bury those of their comrades who were washed ashore. There are two tumuli on the beach at Novgaon. These are believed to be Bene Israel burial mounds—one for the males and the other for the females. Near them stands a monument, a memorial to the arrival of the Bene Israel on the soil of India. In this shipwreck the Bene Israel lost all their belongings including their religious articles.

The small group of survivors (believed to be seven couples) took up the profession of oil pressing. As Saturday is the day of rest for Jews, the Bene Israel ceased work on that day which meant that they did not press or sell oil. As a result the locals called them "Shanwar Telli" (Saturday Oilmen).[12]

The Bene Israel spread from Novgaon to other villages in the Konkan.[13] The names of these villages are known as the Bene Israel (even those living in Israel) still use the names of the villages as their surnames. These are Novgaokars from the village of Novgaon; Kurulkars from the village of Kurul; Sankars

---

12. To this day there is a custom in Maharastra not to buy oil on Saturday. This custom could be traced back to the days when the Bene Israel were "Shanwar Telli" in the villages of the Konkan.
13. In what was called the Kolaba District and is now called Reigad.

from the village of San; Penkars from the village of Pen; and so on. In all, the Bene Israel lived in some 142 villages in the Konkan. There are also Cheulkars—and this "kar" is of historical significance.

It is possible that the Bene Israel were heading for Cheul when the shipwreck took place. Cheul (Chemul) was an important seaport and emporium of trade in ancient times frequented by Arabians, Persians, Egyptians, and other ancient mariners. It was almost certainly the "Simulla" or "Timoula" of Ptolemy (150 C.E.). Some centuries after this date, Cheul declined as a seaport and got silted over. This decline of Cheul is given as the possible explanation as to why the Bene Israel got cut off for centuries from their coreligionists elsewhere and remembered only the basic tenets of Judaism—the Sabbath, circumcision, and the prayer, "Hear O Israel, God our Lord, God is One" (Shema Yisrael). In place of Cheul, Revdanda developed as an important town in the Konkan. However, there are no Revdandakars among the Bene Israel even though there were Bene Israel families living there. There are also no Alibagkars among the Bene Israel even though Alibag is surrounded by villages where the Bene Israel lived. Revdanda and Alibag[14] are comparatively recent creations: The villages of India, to quote Mahatma Gandhi, are from time immemorial. The Cheulkars are indeed witnesses to the antiquity of the Bene Israel.

The first written reference to the Bene Israel is in the twelfth century. The Bene Israel have a rich oral tradition. They also have an historian—Haim Samuel Kehimkar. His family came originally from the Konkan village of Kehim but he lived in Mumbai. He did much to advance the education of the Bene Israel. His book, *The History of the Bene Israel of India*, is accepted as the source book of Bene Israel historical memories. He completed it in 1897 but it was published years later, in 1937, in Tel Aviv through the good offices of Dr. Immanuel Olsvanger, the Zionist emissary to India.[15]

---

14. Revdanda received its name from the Marathas in 1793 (see Shirley Berry Isenberg's *India's Bene Israel*, Popular Prakashan, Bombay, 1988, p. 26). Alibag is said to be called after Ali, a rich Muslim who lived in the seventeenth century. (See Gazetteer of the Bombay Presidency, Kolaba District, originally printed in 1883 and later reprinted at the Government Photozincographic Press, Pune, 1989).

15. (1888–1961). He picked up the manuscript during his first visit to India in 1936.
(Contd.)

Kehimkar relates that some nine hundred years ago a man called Rahabi visited the Bene Israel. He gave the Bene Israel women fish to cook and when he saw that they cooked only the fish with fins and scales he knew they were Jews.[16] He then started the process of bringing them back into mainstream Judaism. This story was dismissed by historians. In fact, the Bene Israel were ridiculed for having mixed up this Rahabi with another Rahabi from Cochin who visited them centuries later. In any case, at that time historians tended to dismiss oral tradition or "folk memory" as myth and legend.

Then came the discovery in 1899 of the "Geniza" in the ancient synagogue at Fustat, the old capital of Egypt, near Cairo. The discoveries of the "Geniza" and later the Dead Scrolls are two great events in recent Jewish history. It is the custom of Jews never to tear up or burn holy writings; they bury them. For some unknown reason the members of this synagogue at Fustat stored documents.[17] The bulk of the contents of the "Geniza" was shipped to Cambridge University in England where to this day research is still being carried out on the documents. A letter was found in the "Geniza" written by David, the brother of the great mediaeval Jewish scholar, Moses Maimomides.[18] David tells his illustrious brother that he was en route to India.[19] David was known as a merchant dealing with precious stones; that he travelled between Ethiopia and India; and that he was the breadwinner of the family. It was during this trip that David drowned in the Indian Ocean.[20] In a subsequent letter[21] addressed to the Rabbis of Lunel in the south of France and dated either 1199 or 1200, Moses Maimonides wrote:

For a critique of Kehimkar's *History* see Mitch Numark: "Constructing a Jewish Nation in Colonial India: History, Narratives of Discent and the vocabulary of Modernity" (Jewish Social Studies winter 2001, Vol. 7, No. 2).

16. Fish must have fins and scales in order to comply with the Jewish dietary laws.
17. "Geniza" is the Hebrew word for "storeroom", usually a room in a synagogue for storing unwanted books.
18. There is a saying in Hebrew: "From Moses (the Law Giver) to Moses (Maimonides) there was no Moses".
19. No. 42 in S.D. Goitein's *Letters of Medieval Jewish Traders* (Princeton University Press, 1973) p. 207.
20. See *A Treasury of Jewish Letters* edited by Franz Kobler (Ararat, London 1952) Vol. I, pp. 191–193.
21. Ibid, pp. 215–217.

Jews of India know nothing of the Torah, and the laws
none save the Sabbath and circumcision,

As would be expected, the Bene Israel immediately saw this
as a vindication of their oral tradition and particularly of their
historian, Kehimkar. They were supported by David Solomon
Sassoon, the antiquarian, who wrote that this might well refer to
"the ancestors of the present Bene Israel",[22] and Schifra
Strizower, the anthropologist.

As the Jews of Cochin are known to have been
familiar with the Written Law (the Law of Moses), the
prophets, and parts of the Talmud, it is assumed that
Maimonides was referring to the Bene Israel.[23]

The next written reference to the Bene Israel appears in the
Moghul Period. It is known that Akbar wanted his kingdom to
be for all religions and races and that he had a passion for
religious discussions and disputations with all leaders of
religious groups. It is known from sources like the *Dabistan* that
Jews played an active role in these discussions. As the Moghul
Empire extended into the Deccan but not into Kerala, it would be
reasonable to assume that it was representatives of the Bene
Israel who sat in Akbar's "Ibadat Khana" particularly as there is
no evidence of Jews living in the interior of India near Delhi. The
Bene Israel themselves addressed this subject and way back in
1896 in their journal, *The Bene Israelite* (which they published in
both English and Marathi), they quote from an address given by

22. A History of the Jews of Baghdad (1949), note 1, p. 218.
23. "The Bene Israel and the Jewish People", note 6, p. 865, in Salo Wittmayer
    Baron, Jubilee Volume, English section, Vol. I (American Academy of Jewish
    Research) Jerusalem 1975. Strizower wrote *The Children of Israel: the Bene Israel
    of Bombay* (Blackwell, Oxford, 1971). It should be pointed here that the late Prof.
    Walter Fischel, who did pioneer studies of the Jews of Persia and India,
    dismissed the Bene Israel claim as a figment of their imagination in an attempt
    to link themselves with one of Jewry's greatest sages. Fischel, however, has
    been criticised for his dismissiveness and disregard for evidence in the
    "Geniza". H.G. Reissner, who did excellent work on Jewish Demography in
    India, wrote that Maimonides really meant Ethiopia not India. Though people
    in the Middle Ages did confuse Ethiopia with India, Prof. Nathan Katz feels
    that it is unlikely that such a great mind like Maimonides would confuse the
    two particularly, as elsewhere, Maimonides correctly described Hindu notions
    of cattle.

the Maharajah of Jodhpur to Aurangzeb in which the Maharajah says of Akbar:

> He preserved every tribe of men in ease and happiness, whether they were followers of Jesus, or of Moses, of Brahma, or Mohammad.

As there is no evidence of Jews living in Jodhpur at the time to the address, it is assumed that the Maharajah knew of their presence in Akbar's "Ibadat Khana". That these Jews were Bene Israel is attested by the fact that the Maharajah used the words "followers of Moses"—exactly the way the Bene Israel described themselves in former times.[24]

Shivaji, on the other hand, knew of the Bene Israel who claimed they acted as his spies and guarded his fort at Raigarh. It is therefore no surprise that Shivaji mentions Jews in a letter to Aurangzeb:

> He (Akbar) adopted an admirable policy of perfect harmony in relation to all the various sects such as Christians, Jews, Muslims ...... Brahmans and Jain Priests.[25]

The Bene Israel too felt threatened by the bigotry of Aurangzeb and Shivaji was as much their champion as he was of the Hindus. Even now Bene Israel speak with no less fervour than any Hindu in the "Kasba" at Pune when recounting the deeds of Shivaji. Bene Israel families (even in Israel) preserve Maratha swords as heirlooms. There was no reason why the Bene Israel should have been excluded from the Maratha army and navy particularly as it is known that Muslims themselves served in them. Kehimkar, for example, mentions the Bene Israel Churrikars who were Naiks of the Angre fleet. For their services they received land in "inam" and a Sarnad. A Bene Israel called Eloji[26], a poet, was consulted on financial matters and foreign policy by the Angre.[27]

---

24. They disliked being called "Jews". They preferred to be called "Bene Israel", "Israelites" or "followers of Moses". In 1738, the Danish missionary, Sartorius, actually uses "Bene Israel" to describe them.
25. J. Sarkar, *Shivaji and his Times*, London, 1920, pp. 366–7.
26. The Bene Israel had become so much part of Maratha society that they even Indianised their first names. Elijah became Eloji; Samuel, Samaji; Isaac, Isaji; and so on.
27. *The Bene-Israelite*, Vol. 3, April 1, 1896, No. 5.

However, it is as soldiers in the Maratha armies that the evidence is overwhelming. After the defeat of the Maratha's by the British at Wandewash in 1760, it is known that at least six Bene Israel joined the British army. They were the five Divekar brothers and Sardar Ezekial Benjamin Malekar. Twenty years later they took part in the Mysore Wars. It was a well established practice of the British to recruit soldiers from the defeated Indian armies. The British also had an uncanny knack of choosing good soldiers whom they took from what they called the "martial races". The Sikhs are perhaps the classic example of this policy. H.G. Reissner found that by 1837, one thousand (or some 19%) out of a Bene Israel population of 5,255 served in the East India Company Army. A large number of these Bene Israel soldiers rose to the rank of Subedar Major, the highest rank a so-called native soldier could reach in the British army. It is inconceivable that the Bene Israel suddenly became hardened soldiers. All evidence points to their winning their spurs during the Maratha period (1627–1818). The British were astute enough to recognise the Bene Israel as a "martial race".[28]

After 1857, when the British army in India was reorganised, the Bene Israel began to leave the army and move into other professions. It was in the nineteenth century that they began leaving their villages in the Konkan and settling in Mumbai and Poona. By 1948, Bene Israel could also be found in Karachi, Ahmedabad, and Nagpur. A few settled elsewhere including Calcutta. There are now some 5,000 Bene Israel left in India—the majority living in Maharastra. There are some 60,000 Jews of Indian origin living in Israel.

---

28. The Bene Israel pre-date the Israelis as soldiers!

Was the Rahabi of the Bene Israel tradition the brother of the Rambam (Moses Maimonides)?

The Bene Israel of India have a rich oral tradition. This folk or collective memory is preserved in the book written by the historian Haeem Samuel Kehimkar, himself a Bene Israel.[1] A tradition that the book addresses (and still persists to this day) is that a certain Rahabi visited the Bene Israel some nine hundred years ago and started a religious revival. He brought them into mainstream Judaism by teaching them what they did not know or had forgotten. He also appointed teachers to continue his work. Kehimkar writes:

> Although David Rahabi was convinced that the Bene Israel were real descendants of the Hebrews, he still wanted to test them further. He therefore, it is said, gave their women clean and unclean fish to be cooked together; but they promptly singled out the clean fish from the unclean ones, saying that they never used fish that had neither fins nor scales.[2]

Historians generally do not attach much credence to oral tradition. They tend to dismiss it as mere myth and legend. Kehimkar's account suffers the same fate. Professor Walter Fischel writes:

> This first confrontation of the "Bene-Israel" with "outside" Jews (*i.e.* the Cochinis) had far-reaching consequences and led to a transformation of their religious life and to a religious revival in their midst. It found its expression in a "Bene-Israel" tradition

---

1. *The History of the Bene-Israel of India* (Tel Aviv, 1937). The book was written in 1897 and lay in manuscript form until it was published forty years later in Israel through the good offices of Dr. Immanuel Olsvanger.
2. Ibid, p. 41.

according to which a religious awakening was brought about through a learned and pious Jew who had arrived from "Egypt" some "nine-hundred years ago" who was called David Rahabi. This David Rahabi, who loomed so large in the legendary accounts of the "Bene-Israel", was apparently no other than David Rahabi of Cochin of the 18th century.[3]

Two letters of Moses Maimonides (the Rambam) still did not move Fischel to reconsider and admit that perhaps the Bene Israel tradition might even have a grain of truth in it. In the first letter the Rambam wrote that his brother, David, had drowned in the Indian Ocean.[4] In the second, he wrote the following:

Only lately some well-to-do men came forward and purchased three copies of my code which they distributed through messengers, in these countries, one copy for each country. Thus the horizon of these Jews was widened and the religious life in all communities as far as India revived. The Jews of India know nothing of the Torah, and of the laws none save the Sabbath and circumcision.[5]

Fischel's response was to see this as a figment of Bene Israel imagination in an attempt to link themselves with one of Jewry's greatest sages. Basically, Fischel doubted Indian sources and he hinted quite broadly at this in the following passage:

The investigation of the place of India in Jewish history can be put on a sounder foundation and based on more reliable documentary evidence only from the second or European phase in the annals of the Jewish

---

3. Introduction to *The Haggadah of the Bene Israel of India* (Orphan Hospital Ward of Israel, New York, 1968).
4. *A Treasury of Jewish Letters* (ed. Franz Kobler) Vol. 1, (Ararat, London, 1952) p. 192.
5. Ibid, p. 217.

association. This period opened with the coming of
the Europeans to India ...[6].

Prof. Brian Weinstein disagrees with Fischel's dismissal of
holy texts and finds it "odd that professor Fischel did not
recognise the value of Cairo Geniza letters and other materials
which document the activities of Jewish traders in India from the
11th to the 13th centuries"[7].

Dr. H.G. Reissner argues that the Rambam might have had
Ethiopia and the Beta Yisrael in mind rather than India as it was
common in the Middle Ages to confuse the two countries.[8]
However Prof. Nathan Katz and Ellen S. Goldberg observe that
"given that elsewhere the Rambam correctly described Hindu
notions about cattle, it doesn't seem likely that such a great mind
would confuse such disparate cultures. More significantly, the
Rambam's beloved younger brother, David, was very much
involved in the India trade; Maimonides wrote that he was able
to study only because of the hard work and generosity of David.
David perished en route to India in shipwreck in 1169, and in the
last communication between the two brothers, David described
the journey to Malabar he was about to undertake. So it seems
quite unlikely that Maimonides would have confused India with
Ethiopia"[9] Nonetheless Katz and Goldberg are non-committal on
whether the David Rahabi of the Bene Israel was really David
Maimonides.

Schifra Strizower considers Kehimkar's account

> ...... a credible tale. In Judaism what one may or may
> not eat is meticulously defined; it is almost impossible
> for an Orthodox Jew to enjoy a normal diet when
> travelling   unless   he   encounters   Orthodox
> coreligionists during his travels. Rahabi, encountering
> the Bene Israel, naturally tried to ascertain whether
> they observed the rules relating to food. (Indeed, that

---

6. *Cochin in Jewish History: Prolegomena to a History of the Jews in India*, Proceedings
   of the American Academy of Jewish Research, Vol. XXX (American Academy
   of Jewish Research, New York, 1962) p. 37.
7. *Biblical Evidence of Spice Trade between India and the Land of Israel: a Historical
   Analysis* (Indian Historical Review, New Delhi, 2001) Vol. XXVII, No. 1.
8. *Maimonides on India* (India and Israel, October 1948).
9. *The Last Jews of Cochin* (University of South Carolina Press, 1993) p. 303, n. 28.

Rahabi is reported to have tested Bene Israel observance of the rules relating to fish seems to me to add credence to the tale; it is extremely difficult to test observance of the rules relating to meat, but comparatively easy to establish whether the rules relating to fish are observed).[10]

Further down she adds that "as the Jews of Cochin are known to have been familiar with the Written Law (The Law of Moses), the prophets, and parts of the Talmud, it is assumed that Maimonides is referring to the Bene Israel". David Solomon Sassoon is also of the opinion that the Rambam "may very well refer to the ancestors of the present Bene Israel".[11]

This paper attempts to show that there is enough circumstantial evidence to confirm the Bene Israel tradition that a Rahabi might well have visited them some nine hundred years ago.

Devora and Menachem Hacohen cogently put forward the Bene Israel position:

A single individual reinvigorated the Bene Yisrael, to an extent that his name became legend in their annals. David Rahabi was a merchant. In the port of Chaoul he learned about the existence of a strange tribe called "shanabar talis" which observed what were obviously Jewish customs and traditions. His curiosity took him to Kunkan (sic). From what he gathered as he talked with them, he realized that he had come upon an ancient tribe. The paucity of its Jewish content was a challenge: he undertook to teach them the Torah and its commandments, as observed in the Jewish world.

Rahabi evidently came from Egypt (Rahab is a name given to Egypt in Jewish liturgical poetry). Some scholars identify him with Rabbi David, brother of Maimonides, a merchant who met his death in shipwreck. Rabbi David, they contend traveled as far as India and was the source of Maimonides'

---

10. *The Bene Israel and the Jewish People* in Salo Wittmayer Baron Jubilee Volume (American Academy for Jewish Research, Jerusalem 1975) Vol. 1, English Section, p. 864.

11. *A History of the Jews of Baghdad* (1949) p. 218, n. 1.

knowledge about the life of Jews there, which he
described in his letter to the sages of Lunel. At any
rate, the visit of David Rahabi implanted in the Bene
Yisrael community much of what remained of
Judaism among them in succeeding centuries.[12]

Cheul (Chemul) was an important seaport and emporium of
trade in ancient times frequented by Arabians, Persians,
Egyptians, and other ancient mariners. It was almost certainly
the "Simulla" or "Timoula" of Ptolemy (150 C.E.). Some
centuries after this date, Cheul silted over and declined as a
seaport. This decline of Cheul is given as the possible explanation
as to why the Bene Israel got cut off for centuries from their
coreligionists elsewhere. However, after the decline of what came
later to be called Lower Cheul, there developed an Upper Cheul
which was named Revdanda by the Marathas in 1763. If Rahabi
came to the Konkan he would have disembarked at Upper Cheul
or Revdanda. There he would certainly have met the Cheulkars
as this was (and still is) a Bene Israel surname. The Bene Israel
would have called him Rahabi not because that was his surname
but because he came from Egypt.[13] In other words he would have
been called "David, the Egyptian" or "David, from Egypt". This
Rahabi cannot therefore have been confused with another David
Rahabi who visited the Bene Israel much later as the latter
belonged to the well-known Rahabi family of Cochin.
Furthermore the Bene Israel tradition clearly states that the
"David, from Egypt" appointed three "Kajis" to be teachers and
preachers in the community something that would be expected
to come from a man from Eygpt as "Kaji" is an Arabic term
meaning judge. As Isenberg has pointed out: "If the 18th century
David Rahabi of Cochin had instituted this Bene Israel office,
why would he have given it a Muslim designation?" He "would
supposedly have preferred a Hebrew title for the persons who
were to learn Hebrew and were to be the religious guides among
the Bene Israel".[14]

---

12. *One People, The Story of the Eastern Jews* (Sabra Books, New York, 1969) pp. 173
    and 174.
13. A biblical example of this is *Elijah the Tishbite (in Hebrew, Eliahoo, the man from
    Tishbeh in Gilead).*
14. *India's Bene Israel* (Popular Prakashan, Bombay, 1988) p. 45.

The Bene Israel tradition not only distinguishes clearly between the two Rahabis but it is also aware of what became of them in the end. Kehimkar says that the Cochin Rahabi was "killed by a local chief two or three years after the commencement of his good work amongst the Bene Israel; and it is said that his grave is in the village called Sarul near Alibag".[15] The Egyptian Rahabi, it appears, is remembered by the Bene Israel in a ceremony that takes place annually in August and is peculiar to the Konkan. A graphic description of this ceremony is given by Maria Graham:

> With one procession, however, I was much pleased; it took place a month ago, on the breaking of the monsoon, when the sea became open for navigation. It is called the coco-nut (sic) feast, and is, I believe, peculiar to this coast. About an hour before sunset, an immense concourse of people assembled on the esplanade, where booths were erected, with all kinds of commodities for sale. All the rich natives appeared in their carriages, and the display of pearls and jewels was astonishing. At sunset, one of the chief Bramins advanced towards the sea, and going out a little way upon a ledge of rock, he launched a gilt coco-nut, in token that the sea was now become navigable; immediately thousands of coco-nuts were seen swimming in the bay; for every priest and every master of a family was eager to make his offering. The evening closed, as usual, with music, dancing, and exhibitions of tumblers, jugglers, and tame snakes.[16]

When the Bene Israel throw their coconuts into the sea they do so for quite a different reason—in remembrance of a holy man who drowned. This ceremony is for them a death anniversary (or "yahrzeit"). Instead of gathering round a tomb and placing stones, they congregate by the sea and throw coconuts on a watery grave.[17]

15. Kehimkar, *op. cit.*, pp. 41 and 42.
16. *Journal of a Residence in India* (Edinburgh, 1813) p. 35.
17. The fact that the Bene Israel are not aware of who exactly the holy man was does not make this custom questionable. They, like other Jewish communities,

(Contd.)

Just as much as the Bene Israel did not mix up the identities of the two Rahabis, the Rambam did not confuse India with Ethiopia. Throughout its history, the Konkan witnessed an influx of Ethiopians well before the establishment of the Sidis at Janjira in the 15th century. There are, for example, depictions of Ethiopians at the ancient caves of Ellora and Ajanta. The Ethiopian presence in the Konkan was felt to such an extent that the area was also called "Habsan", Indian for Abyssinia, Ethiopia's old name.[18] The ruler at Janjira was called by the Bene Israel the "King of Habsan". If the Rambam's reference to Jews in India cannot be accepted at face value, surely it can be argued that the Ethiopia he had in mind was the Indian "Habsan". If this were the case then there can be no doubt that he was thinking exclusively about the Bene Israel and not any other Indian Jewish community. If, however, the Rambam was indeed thinking of Ethiopia proper, it is strange he made no mention of ritual purity. All accounts of the Beta Israel (once called derogatorily "Falashas") note their quite unique practice of placing menstruating women in outhouses. On the other hand, the Rambam's statement aptly describes the Bene Israel religious practice in the 12th century, namely, that they knew nothing of Torah as they lost their Torah scrolls when their ancestors were shipwrecked off the coast of India; their strict observance of the Sabbath earned them the epithet "Shanwar Tellis" (Saturday Oilmen); and they practised circumcision.

The Bene Israel historian, Benjamin J. Israel, believes that the Rambam was referring to the Bene Israel as "his description agrees so closely with that given by Sartorius almost seven centuries later"[19] In 1738 the Danish missionary J.A. Sartorius actually uses the words "Bene Israel", the first known record of the name. He then goes on to say that "they have not the books of the Old Testament"; they "make use of the word 'Shema' as a formula of prayer or doctrine"; and that they "practice circumcision as a part of their religion".[20] Adriaan

still keep customs even though they have forgotten the reason for them. It is the job of the historian to jog their memory; help them to remember; and find historical meaning in their customs.

18. *Gazetteer of the Bombay Presidency, Kolaba District* (Pune, 1989) translates "Habsan" as "African's land".
19. *The Bene Israel of India* (Apt Books, New York, 1984) p. 85.
20. Fischel, *The Haggadah of the Bene Israel, op. cit.*

Moens, the Dutch Governor of Cochin (1771–81), says much the same thing:

> Some miles to the north of Bombay there dwell black men who call themselves Israelites and observe circumcision and also the Sabbath but no other customs or laws.[21]

Nonetheless B.J. Israel is not completely satisfied. He adds:

> What still puzzles me is why Maimonides wrote in such general terms when he must have known that there were Jews in Malabar further south, who knew and observed all the minutiae of the Halacha. Is it possible that some time before Maimonides wrote, the Bene Israel were 'discovered' by Cochinis or even by foreign traders and that the discovery became known to Maimonides?[22]

The question posed can only be described as inspired. Besides Rabbi David Maimonides who was a trader in precious stones, the Rambam could have heard about the Bene Israel from other traders involved in the India trade. He speaks of "well-to-do men" and traders could certainly be included in this category. There are documents in the Cairo Geniza on one such trader—Abraham ben Yiju. He was born in Tunisia and lived in India from at least 1132–1149. He had an export-import business and ran a bronze factory. There is a possibility that he had among his workers in the factory local Jews who might even have been Bene Israel. On his return, Ben Yiju settled in Egypt at its old capital Fustat. His son-in-law Perahya and Perahya's brother Samuel had various contacts with the Rambam who

---

21. Quoted in Isenberg, *op. cit.*, p. 49. The fact that the Bene Israel still practised the basic tenets of Judaism well after the visit of the first Rahabi lends added weight to the argument that this man might well have been David Maimonides. His untimely death was not only a disaster for his brother the Rambam but also, it appears, for the Bene Israel in that he could not complete his work. The signs are that he could have drowned soon after he "discovered" them.

22. *The Bene Israel of India, op. cit.*, p. 85.

himself arrived in Fustat in 1168.[23] With David and the Ben Yiju family as his possible informants, there was no need for the Rambam to specifically mention the Bene Israel as their presence in India was by then probably common knowledge.

In conclusion, the evidence (though mainly circumstantial) points to David Maimonides as being the Rahabi of the Bene Israel and that the Rambam had this community in mind and not the Beta Israel of Ethiopia when he wrote his letter to the Rabbis of Lunel in 1199 or 1200.[24]

---

23. S.D. Goitein and M.A. Friedman: "Abraham Ben Yiju, A Jewish trader in India" (in Hebrew) "Teuda" (Univ. of Tel Aviv, 5759) pp. XXV–XXVII and p. 259 onwards. It is possible that Ben Yiju's grandfather also called Yiju, might have been a Bene Israel who settled in Tunisia. Yiju is a name common among the Bene Israel and is the Marathi equivalent of Ezekiel.
24. Much to the chagrin of the Bene Israel Nathan Katz, in his "An Annotated Bibliography about Indian Jews" places Kehimkar's book in the category of "general interest piece"; not "primary" or "scholarly"! (See Special Bibliography Issue, "Kol Bina", Vol. 8, No. 1, June 1991, New York).

New Evidence on
Samaji Hassaji Divekar

The Bene Israel tradition of how their first synagogue Shaar HaRachamim (Gate of Mercy) came to be founded in 1796 at Mumbai has been difficult to accept as the dates and events associated with its founder, Samaji Hassaji Divekar, are subject to debate. The late Shirley Berry Isenberg summed it up succinctly:

> The actual date of Samaji's imprisonment and of his release from prison still remains a problem.[1]

The Bene Israel tradition has best been related by Shellim Samuel:

> Samuel Ezekiel Divekar, while serving under General Matthews in the Second Mysore War, was taken prisoner by Tippu Sultan and condemned to be beheaded along with other prisoners, but was saved through the intervention of Tippu's mother who was glad to see face to face a 'Banu Israel' so much talked about in the Holy Koran. After two years imprisonment Samuel was released. In gratitude he built the Synagogue at his own expense endowing it with land, to make good his vow made when he was brought to Tippu's court to hear his death warrant.[2]

Documents found in the Pune Archives[3] not only solve the problems posed by Isenberg and others but also attest to the accuracy of the Bene Israel tradition.

Charles Malet, the British Resident in Pune, in correspondence addressed to the Governor-General at Kolkata and dated July 7, 1786, wrote:

---

1. Isenberg: *India's Bene Israel* (Popular Prakashan, Bombay, 1988) p. 318.
2. Brenda Joseph: "Samaji's Synagogue: Tales and Traditions" in *Jews in India* (Ed. Thomas A. Timberg) Vikas Publishing House, New Delhi, 1986, p. 364.
3. There are 73 files of Poona Residency Correspondence (1786–1818) in the Archives.

On the 1st instant my people brought me a person
who had been Jummaadar (sic) in one of the many
Bombay Battalions and was taken prisoner with
General Matthews.[4]

Two days later Malet wrote the following to the Governor of
Bombay:

One Commander, 2 Subadars, 2 Jumaadars (sic) and 2
Englishmen having come here from Tippoo's Army I
have desired Lieutenant Hiern[5] to supply   them
money enough for the necessary expences (sic) and
dispatch them to Bombay with a letter to the
Commanding Officer of the troops.[6]

Then in further correspondence with the Governor-General
dated July 31, 1786, Malet added:

I have the honour to enclose copy of my last address
of the 7th instant. On that day Shamajee Hasajee
Commdt. 2 Subhedars (sic), 2 Jamadars of the Bombay
establishment and 2 Englishmen all of whom had
been detained on the pacification and since enlarged
on consenting to enter into Tippoo's service arrived
here having made their escape with great peril and
difficulty from the army near Adoni. The Commander
whom I found to be very observant and shrewd man
confirms every part of the other Jamadar's
information as communicated in my last letter and
gives some additional detail of which I have taken the
liberty of troubling the Governor General.[7]

In a communication dated August 11, 1786, Malet gave some
details of how the escapes were made:

Amidst the confusion that prevailed on his (Tipu's)
hasty retreat from before Adoni many black officers

---

4. Poona Residency Correspondence, File No. 1, p. 44.
5. Subsequently his name is spelt "Hurn".
6. Poona Residency Correspondence, File No. 1, p. 253.
7. Ibid, p. 57.

and sepoys belonging to Bombay who had been detained on the general release at the pacification made their escape and have passed this route to Bombay..............[8]

As can be seen, these documents confirm by and large Shellim Samuel's account. However, just one sentence needs to be altered for it to be fully accurate: "After two years imprisonment Samuel was released" should be replaced by "After two years serving Tipu Sultan, Samuel escaped".

The documents also throw light on another aspect of Bene Israel history. Shellim Samuel's account mentions "other prisoners". These other prisoners included some Bene Israels. How many is not clear.[9] Besides Samaji Hassaji, two Sankars are mentioned in a document[10]—one a carpenter and another a mender of utensils,[11] both in the Commissary's Department. Of the two Subedars who escaped, one was probably Subedar Major Sardar Bahadur Ezekiel Benjamin Malekar.[12] The other Subedar and the two Jamadars could well be Bene Israel but what their names were are not revealed by any document. What can reasonably be assumed is that there were at least six other Bene Israel prisoners with Divekar.

A Postscript

The claim that Divekar was released as a result of the intervention of a member of the Rahabi family of Cochin is not supported by the documents. In any case the Bene Israel historian, Benjamin J. Israel, considered it as "open to doubt in many respects" and that "the Bene Israel tradition is more plausible, even if the intervention of Tipu Sultan's mother is discounted" (*The Bene Israel of India*, Apt Books, New York, 1984).

---

8. Ibid, p. 208, Malet to Sir Archibald Campbell.
9. Ezekiel Barber speaks of "several" (p. 49, "The Bene-Israel of India," University Press of America, 1981).
10. Poona Residency Correspondence, File No. 12, p. 310, Cherry to Tipu Sultan March 19, 1793. The British still believed that Tipu held prisoners taken with General Matthews.
11. The Marathi "siccaulghur" is used. Though the Sankars are spelt "Sunker" and "Sunkar" it is reasonable to suppose that they were Bene Israel.
12. I.A. Ezekiel's article "Martial Traditions of the Bene-Israel Community" in the journal "India and Israel", February 1949, No. 8,.

ART

Professor David's Collections include Historic Treasure from India

An important historical document has been found among a pile of private papers that has been lying in a storeroom in the Israel Museum in Jerusalem since 1969. It reads:

> In this collection there are several manuscripts and miniatures/paintings of the first importance which formerly belonged to the Imperial Library of the Moghul Emperors of India, at Delhi, which Nādir Shāh carried away as spoils of war to Persia. That booty included the famous diamond which he called Kūh-i-Nūr, that is, 'the mountain of light', and today adorns the crown of our Queen; and the Peacock Throne is still in Teheran.[1]

The collection is the "Dawūd Collection" which consists of rare paintings and artefacts mainly from the Islamic world. In 1984 it was valued at, at least, twenty million pounds sterling.[2] As originals they are in fact priceless.[3]

Next door at the Hebrew University there is the Yochanan ben David Collection of books and Persian and Arabic manuscripts.[4] In a letter of thanks to the donor the then Acting Librarian, D.H. Baneth, wrote in 1946:

1. These treasures were taken by Nadir Shah in 1739–40.
2. Article, Jerusalem Post, 24.8.1984.
3. The only other comparable collection still in private possession is the Queen of England's Indian miniatures at the Windsor Royal Library which illustrate the *Padshanama* (Chronicle of the King of the World).
4. The Jewish National and University Library at the Hebrew University lists it as the "Ben-David, Yochanan: Collection dedicated to the memory of Yekutiel Ben-David, London, 1937". Yekutiel, a *Hakim* (doctor), was the brother of Yochanan. He died in Israel in 1935. The late Prof. Walter Fischel in an article *The University and the Fabled East*, referred to the Dawūd bequest as "outstanding" (*The New Palestine*, July 13, 1945, p. 248, Washington, U.S.A.).

.... Exquisite bindings and perfect penmanship further enchance the value of many manuscripts and books. Apart from that we found artistic calligraphic specimens and interesting nail-prints ..... This is the second collection our Library was favoured with by you .... Your two contributions which belong to the best and most interesting collections we ever received, are valuable and important addition to our Oriental Department. We are indeed grateful for your generosity.[5]

Few know that the Dawūd of the pictures and the ben David of the books and manuscripts are one and the same person—Mirza Yuhanna Dawūd Khan in Persian; Yohanan ben David in Hebrew; Professor John David in English. Mirza and Khan are titles.[6]

Since his boyhood, Prof. David collected fine Persian works of art and Islamic treasures which, he wrote, include some "historical pieces" and "valuable objects of great interest". He continued:

Some of these masterpieces have been executed by famous Persian artists, and Islamic masters, for the Persian Shahs; the Sultans of Turkey; the rulers of Egypt and the Moghul Emperors of India. When these works of oriental art are examined by art experts, they will prove beyond dispute their great value, and to be

5. Nail-prints are prints drawn with the fingernails. The presentation of books was made in 1925 when Lord Balfour opened the Hebrew University. In all, ben-David presented 1055 volumes, 50 of which were Arabic and Persian manuscripts. All these have an "Ex Libris" in Hebrew and signed also in Hebrew, Yohanan ben David. Dawūd came from a religious background and it appears was himself a traditional Jew. His papers usually have written at the top right hand corner a blessing in Hebrew, and photographs of himself have the Hebrew word "Hazair" (the young) before his name—apparently both common practices among the Persian Jews. Another Persian Jew, Mulla Ibrahim Nathan (1816–1868) appears in Hebrew as "Hazair Abraham Nathan" (see Fischel, *Mulla Ibrahim Nathan*, Hebrew Union College Annual, Vol. XXIX, 1958, p. 364). The source for the use of "hazair", Persian Jews point out, is the *Book of Job* where it signifies a deference to others (Ch. 32.6).
6. Mirza is a Persian title meaning "born a prince". However, since the time of Nadir Shah, it has been applied to a literate person. Khan is a Turkish title meaning princely.

unrivalled throughout the whole countries of the Near and Middle East. They are exceedingly rare, and could not be possible to purchase, at any price, any more.[7]

Prof. David was born on April 6, 1884, at Kermanshah in Persia. His father, Jacob, had the title *Khwadja*. Sir Moses Montefiore had written letters to him enquiring about the state of affairs of the Persian Jews.[8] He was a personal friend of Lord Curzon.[9] Prof. David wrote:

My ancestors for many generations had important appointments at the Persian Royal Mint, first at Teheran, and afterwards at Kermanshah, where I was born; and according to our family records or history, my father also filled this appointment at the Royal Mint for many years with credit to himself and to the Persian nation which was wise enough to appreciate his honesty, as well as his genius, as gold refiner or Tizabi—which is our family surname to this day ..... My forefathers for many generations enjoyed a great privilege of that country (Persia), believing to be of the seed of David, they were known as Ibn-i-Dawūd.[10]

In 1906, Prof. David went to Pembroke College, Cambridge University, where he worked with the distinguished Persian scholar and author—Professor Edward Browne.[11] In July 1909, he

---

7. One famous painter was the court painter of Shah Abbas II (1642–1667)—Muhammad Zamān. Zamān became a protégé of the Moghul Emperor Shah Jahan, the builder of the Taj Mahal.
8. Khwadja is an honorific title generally borne by ministers of sovereigns who were chosen from among the learned. In 1860, there was a drought in Persia (see Avraham Cohen: *The Jewish Community In Kermanshah* 1992).
9. Lord Curzon (1859–1925) was Viceroy of India, Chancellor of Oxford University, and Foreign Secretary of Britain, in that order.
10. His teacher and friend was Haji Malak-ul-Kalam who later became Chancellor of the University of Teheran and Persian Minister of Education. Another friend was his Imperial Highness, Prince Salar-ud-Dawlah, of the Qajar Dynasty.
11. Edward Graville Browne, eminent British Iranologist (1862–1926). Miss Jayne Ringrose, the Pembroke College Archivist, in a communication kindly passed on to the author of this article by Sir Roger Tomkys, Master of the College, drew attention to the existence of "a number of courses at Cambridge at the end of the nineteenth and beginning of the twentieth century in preparation for various branches of foreign service for Britain and other countries (for
(Contd.)

was selected to go to Schaffhausen in Switzerland to decipher and translate into English a number of oriental inscriptions. Whilst there he wrote several large works on oriental art, arms and armour, which were published in English, French, and German. In 1913, he became a naturalized British subject and, during the First World War, worked with Sir Denison Ross at the War Office and in the Censors Office.[12] Later he translated into English important Arabic and Persian manuscripts which exist in the Libraries of the British Museum, India Office, Royal Asiatic Society as well as the Libraries on the continent of Europe. He also had access to private art collections including that of Baron Edmond de Rothschild of Paris.

With such a background, it comes as something of a surprise to learn that Prof. David was unknown to the Israeli

example, the Levant Consular Service including the Student Interpreters, the Indian Civil Service, and that of other Eastern countries, the British Foreign Service, and various others from time to time). Anything involving near Eastern languages came under the aegis of E.G. Browne, whose rooms functioned as kind of headquarters for those students. Lectures were given in Pembroke and Peterhouse .... Sir Reader Bullard's autobiography, *The Camels Must Go* (London, 1961) describes (pp. 45–49) the life of a Student Interpreter who was taught by E.G. Browne".

According to Dr. Jonathan Holmes, the Archivist of Queens' College, Cambridge, where Reader Bullard was a Student Interpreter from 1906 to 1908, Bullard was a member of the College but did not take a degree. As Dawūd was not a member of Pembroke it is unlikely he went up to Cambridge as a Student Interpreter. He could have gone up as an independent student under the patronage of Prof. Browne. However, there is a reference in his private papers to his having "worked with" Prof. Browne suggesting that he went to Cambridge not as a student but in some other capacity—an assistant to Browne perhaps.

Dr. John Gurney of Wadham College, Lecturer in Persian at Oxford University, who is working on   a biography of Prof. Browne, has found references to Dawūd in Browne's papers. Browne described him as "a Persian Baha'i Jew". Prof. David donated several manuscripts to the British Museum including Baha'i ones. These are mainly listed in the Persian handlist of the British Library for 1895-1966. The Archives at the Baha'i World Centre at Haifa in Israel has material on Dawūd. The report on Dawūd's marriage (see next section *From the Archives*) was given to the author by the Centre.

12. Sir Denison later became Director of the School of Oriental (now Asian-African) Studies, University of London. This is an example of how the British used academics to assist in the war effort. Prof. David was used again in World War II by the Ministry of Information to write articles in Persian in its quarterly cultural magazine, *Ruzgar-i naw*. The articles included a "Great British Orientalists" series which was passed by another distinguished Cambridge Iranologist, also from Pembroke, Prof. Arberry. (Thanks to Muhammad Isa Waley, Head of Persian and Turkish Collections at the British Library, for his assistance).

establishment. He was the "spy who loved art" and "a very strange man whose real name we don't even know".[13] Two major exhibitions were held in Israel featuring paintings from his Collection. On both occasions books were published under the auspices of the Israel Museum.[14] However, in a Preface to one of the books,[15] Prof. David's name and year of birth were recorded wrongly and he was described as being of a "middle-class Jewish family", "not a religious Jew", nor an "active Zionist".[16]

Prof. David was known to most of the Professors and learned institutions in England, France, Switzerland, America, and elsewhere. He held exhibitions of his Collection at the Royal Academy, London, in 1931, and the City of Manchester Art Gallery in the same year.[17] He was Curator of the Department of Islamic Art at the British Museum and in his time was considered the foremost expert in Great Britain in this field. In 1938, his Collection was reviewed in the prestigious Hyderabad Quarterly Review in India—*Islamic Culture*.[18]

Prof. David's wish was to come to Israel with his Collection:

> My chief intention of immigrating to Israel is to be of some service to out noble Brethren, who have re-built our Holy Land, and to work with my learned friends, for the good understanding and friendship between the Arabs and the Israelis. I believe that this axiomatic object should be achieved through the medium of cultural pursuits and not by guns and bombs. We are

13. ERETZ magazine, Spring 1992. See also Aharon Meggid's article in "Yediot Ahranot", 18.8.1984.
14. Rachel Milstein: *Islamic Paintings in the Israel Museum* (Israel Museum, Jerusalem, 1984); and Na'ama Brosh with Rachel Milstein: *Biblical Stories in Islamic Painting* (Sabinsky Press Ltd., Tel Aviv, 1991).
15. *Biblical Stories in Islamic Painting.*
16. The former Director of the Israel Museum in Jerusalem, Dr. Martin Weyl, in a letter written before he left office, assured the author of this paper that "we have taken heed" that some kind of official correction be made in fairness to Dawūd who has enriched the cultural life of Israel.
17. His art treasures were also exhibited at the Bodleian Library, Oxford University, which also received from him Hebrew, Persian, Arabic, and Turkish manuscripts in 1937 and again in 1962. (Thanks to Richard Judd and Colin Wakefield of the Department of Oriental Books for their assistance in locating these).
18. Volume XII, 1938, pp. 365–267. He himself wrote an article on "The Amery Collection of Persian Paintings" (Indian Art and Letters 16, New Series, 1942) pp. 90–92 (L.S. Amery was Secretary of State for India).

closely akin racially with the Arabs. The Hebrew and
Arabic languages are sister tongues.[19]

Yochanan ben David, Professor of Oriental Art and
Literature, oriental translator and art expert, did not come to
Israel with his Collection. His Collection did. He himself died in
London in 1969 and his body was not brought to Israel for burial.

**Catalogue of books in David Collection at the National Library
at the Hebrew University, Givat Ram, Jerusalem (V 1288)**

(NB. dates in C.E. (A.D.). A.H. refers to the Islamic Calendar.
Comments by Prof. David).

1. "The flower-bed of Ibrahim". A poem on Ibrahim Adham
   (1087 A.H.)
2. The complete works of Hafiz written in excellent Shikasta
   and illuminated with four double page Sarlouhs (1728).
3. "The garden of Truth"—a philosophical work written in
   Taliq within gold rules (early 16th. century) A very
   important and rare work.
4. History of Alexander the Great in Persian verse by Nizami
   (probably 15th century).
5. Zigi-Ullugh Beg; the astronomical canons and tables of the
   celebrated Eastern astronomer Sultan Ullugh Beg, grandson
   of Taymur (1421).
6. The code of laws made by Shah Abbas the Great. Written in
   Nastaliq and copied from an older Ms. in 1834.
7. History of Nadir Shah written in Nastaliq (1827).
8. The conquest of Sind—history of Sind from the Muhammadan
   conquest to the annexation by Akbar. Composed by
   Muhammad Masum and written in a neat Nastaliq.
9. Selections from "Mathnawi" of Jala-ud-Din-i-Rumi. One
   page wanting at the end.
10. A collection of select poems and verses from eminent
    Persian poets. Copies by Ibn-i-Ali Katib, a famous Persian
    calligraphist (1565).

---

19. Prof. David visited Israel in 1926. A record of that trip is in the Manuscript
    Department of the Hebrew University at Givat Ram in Jerusalem. One entry
    in the diary reads as follows:
    "I believe in my inmost heart that Zionism is essentially the cause of G-d,
    and the upbuilding of the Jewish National Home in Palestine is the purpose of
    the Almighty which man can help but cannot hinder".

11. Arabic Ms. Prayers attributed to Ali with Persian translation in verse. Copied by the slave, Mir Husayn al-Husayni of Bukhara, at Mecca (probably 15th century).
12. Gulistan of Sadi, finely written in Nastaliq at Tihran, Persia.
13. Anwar-i-Suhayli the Persian translation of Kalilah Wa-Dimanah, a very elegant paraphrase of Pilpai's tales and fables by Husayn Ibn-i-Ali Al-Waizal-Kashifi (1793).
14. Bustan-i-Sadi, moral stories in Persian verse. Copyist: Haydar Ali Beg (1802).
15. The Seeker's Guide to Truth; a philosophical work written in fine Naskh (18th century).
16. A universal guide with numerous Arabic quotations. Persian Ms. dated 1857. Copyist: Ismail. A most interesting and valuable work of its kind.
17. The memoirs of the Persian poets by Dawlatshah Ben Ala-ud-Dawlah Al-Samarqandi (1487). Written in fine Nastaliq by Khalil-ullah Al-Katib (1564).
18. Selections from general history by Bakhityar Khan. A few lines missing at the end.
19. Persian Ms. consisting of three treatises:
The flowerbed of Ibrahim
The crown of Ibrahim
The letter of Nawras
Written in excellent Nastaliq (1875).
20. The burning and melting. A Sati episode composed by Mullah Nani. Written in clear Indian Nastaliq (this was translated into English by Mirza Y. Dawud of Persia and Ananda Coomaraswamy of Ceylon in 1912).
21. Selected remarks on the science of Astronomy—mostly treating of astrological observations. A Persian Ms. written in clear Nastaliq. Persian Cashmere binding (1839).
22. Some questions relative to the Hadith and legends of Muhammadanism written in Indian Taliq (1804).
23. An Arabic treatise on the nature and watering of swords composed by the celebrated Arabian philosopher, Yaqub Ben Ishaq Al-Kindi. Copied from a unique Ms. in the library of Leyden in 1910 with a Persian translation by Mirza Yakutiel Dawud, Prof. David's brother, in 1911.

24. The forty wise sayings of Ali written in excellent Naskh with Persian translation in verse. Copied by Muhammad the Scribe (1579).

25. A Dictionary of Arabic, Turkish, and Persian, written in excellent Naskh by Ismail Ibn-i-Ibrahim Tuirani (1797).

26. Arabic Ms. written in fine Naskh. Scribe: Mirza Muhammad Ibn-i-Mihr Ali of Tamsha (1243 A.H.).

27. Arabic Ms. "Hashiyah-i-Khata" written in Naskh. Sayings and teachings attributed to the early Muhammadan teachers (1196 A.H.). Scribe: Abdul Riza Ibn-i-Ala-ud-Dawla Al Shulistani.

28. Persian Ms. Copies of celebrated letters and sayings written in fine Nastaliq on gold ground.

29. Arabic Ms. A philosophical work written in Naskh (1121 A.H.).

30. Persian Ms. Bahai epistles written in Naskh by Mirza Zain, a Persian calligraphist.

31. Historical notices on two Indian tribes by Abdul Majid Jukhi written in 1851.

32. A Persian Ms. containing Part I and Part II of a moral story written in Nastaliq.

33. Persian Ms. on Cashmere and its famous woollen shawls. Written in Indian Nastaliq. Exceedingly interesting.

34. Arabic Ms. "Evidences". A Sufi work written in excellent Nastaliq (1066 A.H.).

35. Arabic Ms. Prayers attributed to the Hebrew Prophets, Muhammad and Ali. Also invocations with instructions in Turkish for warding off the influence of the evil eye; for cure of diseases; and protection against the enemy (probably 17th century).

36. Album of Arabic calligraphy in Thuluth and Naskh characters. The colophon reads: "Written by Shaykh Hamdullah, known as the Ibnu-Sh-Shaykh who was then a Badha and 80 years old".

37. Arabic Ms. A Sufi work of the highest importance dealing with spiritual travels from the earth to the heavenly places. Written in fine Persian Nastaliq on silk paper. The author is Sadr-ud-Din Shirazi (1239 A.H.).

38. Arabic Ms. dealing with the sciences of numbers by Yahya Ben Ahmad Alkashi. Written in very fine Naskh by the

copyist Shaykh Ismail Ben Abdul Wunab Ben Said Ben Ahmad (925 A.H.).

39. Persian Ms. written in Indian Nastaliq by the copyist Muhammad Zia ul-Haq (1066 A.H.).
40. Arabic Ms. written in good Maghribi character (18th century). Cashmere binding.
41. Arabic Ms. Calligraphy. Wise sayings of the ancient sages written in large and medium Naskh by Abdullah Ar-Rashad (1198 A.H.).
42. Arabic Ms. written in Maghribi character (1154 A.H.). Cashmere binding.
43. Arabic Ms. A treatise on Logic (probably 18th century). Cashmere binding.
44. A collection of Muhammadan teachings and doctrines written in Maghribi character (1151 A.H.). Cashmere binding.
45. Persian Ms. The seven proofs of the Bab in his claim to be the Muhammadan Qaim. Written in clear Nastaliq.
46. A Turkish, Persian, and French vocabulary.

Cat. of Mss.: VAR 109-116; 517; VA 116.3 (nailing).

Manuscripts at the Bodleian Library at Oxford University in England, Dept. of Oriental Books

Dawud, Yuhanna   Card 1

MS. Heb.e.162—5 May 1937
MS. Pers.b.6 (R)—5 May 1937
MS.Pers.c.40, 41—5 July 1962
MS. Pers.d. 76, 77(R)—5 July 1937
MS. Pers.d. 112, 113—5 July 1962
MS. Pers.e.44—Aug. 1920
MS. Pers.e.62, 63—5 May 1937
MS. Pers.e.92—5 July 1962
MS. Pers.f.6 —5 May 1937

Dawud, Yuhanna   Card 2

MS. Arab.a.1(R)–3(R)—5 May 1937
MS. Arab.d.181—5 May 1937
MS. Arab.d.237—5 July 1962
MS. Arab.165–168—5 May 1937
MS. Arab.234, 235—5 July 1962
MS. Turk.e.62-64(R)—5 May 1937

Manuscripts of Dr. Yuhanna Dawud at the British Library, London, England

I.O. 4740 *Aḥvāl-i Muḥammad Shāh pādshāh-i vālājah-i Hind,* a brief account of Nādir Shāh's defeat of the Mughal forces at Karnal in 1739. Ff 1Dr-5v; 23 × 13 cm; seal dated 1192 (1778). Persian.

I.O. 4741 A collection of four short works relating to the Tāj Maḥall at Agra:

(a) An untitled and anonymous work in Urdu prose, probably by Ghulām Imām Shahīd (1804—*c*.1876), giving an account of Mumtāz Maḥall's final illness and last wishes, and the construction of her mausoleum after her death in 1631. (ff 1r—10v). Urdu (See *Urdu mss II* no. 33)

(b) *Dar ta'rīf-i rawzah,* a description in prose and verse of the Tāj Maḥall by Shihāb al-Dīn Muḥammad. (ff 11r—31v). Persian

(c) *Ta'rīf-i rauzah-yi munavvarah,* a prose description forming part of the third chapter of *Tājganj ke rauze kī ta'rīf* by Ghulām Imām Shahīd. (ff 32r—43v). Urdu (See *Urdu mss II* no. 33)

(d) *Khulāṣah-i paymāyish-i rawzah* ... Measurements etc. of the Tāj Maḥall. (ff 45r—67r). Persian
69 ff; 25.5 × 17 cm; late 19th century.

FROM THE ARCHIVES

A Bahá'í Wedding

This account of Prof. David's wedding in 1911 is in the Bahá'í Archives at Haifa, Israel, the World Centre of the movement.

QUITE an oriental note was struck toward the end of 'Abdu'l-Bahá's London visit, by the marriage of a young Persian couple who had sought his presence for the ceremony, the bride journeying from Baghdad accompanied by her uncle in order to meet her fiance here and be married before 'Abdu'l-Bahá's departure. The bride's father and grandfather had been followers of Bahá'u'lláh during the time of his banishment.

We hesitate to alter the bridegroom's description of the service and therefore print it in his own simple and beautiful language. It will serve to show a side not touched on elsewhere, and without which no idea of his visit is complete. We refer to the attitude of reverence with which people from the East who came to see 'Abdu'l-Bahá regard their great teacher. They invariably rise and stand with bowed heads whenever he enters the room.

Mírzá Dáwud writes:—

On Sunday morning, the 1st of October, 1911, A.D., equal to the 9th Tishi 5972[*] (Hebrew Era), Regina Núr Mahal Khánum, and Mírzá Yuhanna Dáwud were admitted into the holy presence of 'Abdu'l-Bahá: may my life be a sacrifice to Him!

After receiving us, 'Abdu'l-Bahá said, "You are very welcome and it makes me happy to see you here in London".

Looking at me he said, "Never have I united anyone in marriage before, except my own daughter, but as I love you much, and you have rendered a great service to the Kingdom of Abhá both in this country and in other lands, I will perform your marriage ceremony today. It is my hope that you may both continue in the blessed path of service".

Then, first, 'Abdu'l-Bahá took Núr Mahal Khánum into the next room and said to her, "Do you love Mírzá Yuhanna Dáwud with all your heart and soul?" She answered, "Yes, I do".

---

[*] Misprint; should read Tishri 5672.

Then 'Abdu'l-Bahá called me to him and put a similar question, that is to say, "Do you love Núr Maḥal Khánum with all your heart and soul"? I answered "Yes, I do". We re-entered the room together and 'Abdu'l-Bahá took the right hand of the bride and gave it into that of the bridegroom and asked us to say after him, "We do all to please God".

We all sat down and 'Abdu'l-Bahá continued; "Marriage is a holy institution and much encouraged in this blessed cause. Now you two are no longer two, but one. Bahá'u'lláh's wish is that all men be of one mind and consider themselves of one great household, that the mind of mankind be not divided against itself.

"It is my wish and hope that you may be blessed in your life. May God help you to render great service to the kingdom of Abhá and may you become a means of its advancement.

"May joy be increased to you as the years go by, and may you become thriving trees bearing delicious and fragrant fruits which are the blessings in the path of service".

When we came out, all the assembled friends both of Persia and London congratulated us on the great honour that had been bestowed upon us, and we were invited to dine by the kind hostess.

After a little while we gathered around the table with him. During the meal one of the friends asked 'Abdu'l-Bahá how he enjoyed his stay in London, and what he thought of the English people. I acted as interpreter. 'Abdu'l-Bahá replied: "I have enjoyed London very much and the bright faces of the friends have delighted my heart. I was drawn here by their unity and love. In the world of existence there is no more powerful magnet than the magnet of love. These few days will pass away, but their import shall be remembered by God's friends in all ages and in all lands.

There are living nations and dead nations. Syria lost its civilization through lethargy of spirit. The English nation is a living one, and when in this spiritual springtime the divine truth come forth with renewed vitality, the English will be like fruitful trees, and the Holy Spirit will enable them to flourish in abundance. Then will they gain not only materially, but in that which is far more important, spiritual progress, which will enable them to render a greater service to the world of humanity".

Another asked why the teachings of all religions are expressed largely by parables and metaphors and not in the plain language of the people.

'Abdu'l-Bahá replied:—"Divine things are too deep to be expressed by common words. The heavenly teachings are expressed in parable in order to be understood and preserved for ages to come. When the spiritually minded dive deeply into the ocean of their meaning they bring to the surface the pearls of their inner significance. There is no greater pleasure than to study God's Word with a spiritual mind".

"The object of God's teaching to man is that man may know himself in order to comprehend the greatness of God. The Word of God is for agreement and concord. If you go to Persia where the friends of Abhá are many, you will at once realize the unifying force of God's work. They are doing their utmost to strengthen this bound of amity. There, people of different nationalities gather in one meeting and chant the divine tablets with one accord. It might be supposed that they were all brethren. We do not consider anyone a stranger, for it is said by Bahá'u'lláh 'Ye are all the rays of one sun; the fruits of one tree; and the leaves of one branch.' We desire the true brotherhood of humanity. This shall be so, and it has already begun. Praise to be God, the Helper, the Pardoner!"

Is Ophir in the Indian Ocean?

This letter was written on November, 11, 1959, to Dr. Olsvanger by Israel's second President, Itzak Ben-Zvi. The original letter is in the "Genizim", the Archives of the Association of Hebrew Writers at Tel Aviv, Israel (41268–aleph). Ben-Zvi was very interested in the oriental Jews and there is now an Institute named after him in Jerusalem. This letter has been translated from the Hebrew.

Regarding your letter of November 6, 1959, on the subject of Burma-Ophir: as you know, there are three opinions about where the land of Ophir, mentioned in the Bible, is situated. But, first and foremost, if someone has doubts of the actual existence of Ophir, surely all these doubts would disappear when one sees the writing on the ostracon at Tel Qasile near Tel Aviv. The writing reads in translation: "Ophir gold for Beth-Horin 30 shekels".

This writing, according to the experts, belongs to the 9th or 8th century (B.C.E.), that is, the period after King Solomon—therefore one learns that not only Solomon brought gold from Ophir but also the Kings of Judah who came after him; in other words, one can assume that from Solomon until Yehoshapat there was constant contact through ships and commerce between Eilat and Etzion Geber and the land of Ophir—and one would assume—also after that.

The three opinions are:

(a) that Ophir was in southern Arabia
(b) that Ophir was on the east coast of Africa
(c) that Ophir was in the Indian Ocean

I don't accept the first two opinions but I accept the third: Ophir is in one of the countries in the Indian Ocean. It is understood that it is difficult to pinpoint precisely whether the exact place intended is India itself, Burma, or another land in the area. Perhaps in order to decide on this, one might have to turn to the world of zoology, botany, or mineralogy, as there are at least seven or eight names that bring to mind the connection with these places.

On this question I had an argument with Prof. Gordon Lewis, an important orientalist and linguist at the University of Rangoon, and an expert in Burmese, Pali, Chinese, etc. He agreed that my assumptions deserve research—he requested taking an interest in the aspect of philology that touches on these two ideas: peacocks, monkeys, sandalwood, ivory, elephants, ebony, silver, gold, and precious stones. It follows that research in the zoological, botanical, and mineral names will give us some kind of key to determine the exact location of Ophir.

I am greatful to you for the three examples you gave me from Sanskrit and the Dravidian languages:

1. KAPI—"monkey" in Sanskrit
2. PILUH—"elephant" in Sanskrit
3. TOGAI-TOGHAI—"peacock" in Dravidian

Together with this one needs to look for examples also in the Akkadian and ancient Semitic languages thus clarifying the point that the sea link between India and Aram-Naharaim was in existence well before King Solomon, about the beginning of the second millennium before the Christian Era.

I have with me two good proofs pointing to Burma and the Malay peninsular:

(a) the name Mount Ophir appears in the Encyclopaedia Britannica as Delacman: Encyclopaedia Britannica: XIII, p. 119: "Johore—a Malayan State at the Southern end of the peninsular. The highest point is Mt. Ophir" (Gunon Ledang, 4, 187 ft.)

(b) the name of the metal "ophir" mentioned in the book of Shlomo Reinemann, "Journeys of Shlomo" (p. 193)

Of course it is worth comparing whether the well-known stone called Opal or Opolous that is derived from the Sanskrit word—"Upala"—has any connection with the name ophir.

In Ben-Yehuda's dictionary it is opined that the stone opal is "leshem".

Regarding your correct observation on the inscription on palm leaves, I did not say that this was special to Burma but that the custom of writing on palm leaves was more widespread in Burma than in other countries. I pointed to examples of the Koran written on palm leaves that are well-known as they appear on the steam engine of one of the Caliphs.

Your assumption with regard to the quotation from Koheleth* certainly appears to me interesting and for this may you be blessed.

Greetings,
(signed) Itzak Ben-Zvi

P.S. Attached to this is the quotation from R.D. Brunt.

---

* Ecclesiastes.

A Note on Kehimkar's *History*

The Bene Israel historian Haeem Samuel Kehimkar in his "History of the Bene Israel of India" (Tel Aviv, 1937) relates the following on page 260 of his book:

> This schism continued for a few years, but it was discontinued as soon as their Muccadam Subedar Sillamonji Bapuji Sankar was stabbed by his brother-in-law, *i.e.*, his wife's sister's husband who was of the family of Pingley; for he the Subedar ill-treated his wife's sister; while he transferred his affection to his own kept woman. This Pingley was hanged in 1836, and this is the only Bene-Israel on record that has been hanged since the Bene-Israel came into Bombay.

This event is recorded in the Criminal Records Vol. No. 36, 1826, at the Mumbai Archives, Elphinstone College:

Tuesday October 17. 1826

Present

The Honble Sir Edward West Knight Chief Justice
The Honble Sir Charles Chambers Knight Puisne Justice

Rex
vs
Eloye Abramjee Israel

The Prisoner is set to the Bar and arraigned upon the following Indictment and Inquisition

In the Supreme Court of Judicature at Bombay
Crown side
Bombay to wit   The Jurors for our sovereign Lord the King upon their oath present That Eloye Abramjee Israel late of Bombay Inhabitant and labourer not having the fear of God before his Eyes, but being moved and seduced by the instigation of the Devil on the twenty third day of august in the seventh year of the Reign of our Sovereign Lord George the Fourth by the Grace of God of
united

Bombay Town Hall Tuesday the 17. day of October 1826

united Kingdom of Great Britain and Ireland King Defender of the faith
with force and arms at Bombay aforesaid within the Jurisdiction of the Supr
-me Court of Judicature at Bombay in and upon one Sooliman Sanker ——
the peace of God and our said Lord the King then and there being feloniously
wilfully and of his Malice aforethought did make an assault and that he
he the said Eloze Abramye Israel with a certain drawn Sword made of
Iron and steel of the value of five Rupees which he the said Eloze &
Abramye Israel in his right hand then and there had and held him
the said Sooliman Sanker in and upon the Belly of him the said
Sooliman Sanker then and there feloniously wilfully and of his malice
aforethought did thrust stab and penetrate giving to the said Sooliman
Sanker then and there with the Sword aforesaid in and upon the aforesaid
Belly of him the said Sooliman Sanker one mortal wound of the breadth
of three Inches and of the Depth of three Inches of which said mortal wound
the said Sooliman Sanker then and there instantly died — and so the
Jurors aforesaid upon their oath aforesaid do say that the said &
Eloze Abramye Israel him the said Sooliman Sanker in the
manner and by the means aforesaid feloniously wilfully and of his
malice aforethought did kill and Murder against the peace of our
said Lord the King his Crown and Dignity

     Plea Non Cul — Prisoner po se   Rep Cul prist

The following Panel not being Challenged are sworn to try the Issue

1	Mr. William Renton	7	Mr. John Caldecott
2	John Ashman	8	George Cadenhead
3	Lewis Collell	9	Nathaniel Spencer
4	Charles Belcour	10	Rodney Kempt
5	Robert Bennett	11	Henry Enderwick
6	John Alexr. Higgs	12	Frances Owen

The Jury are charged with the Indictment & Inquisition
Verdict Guilty of Murder
Judgment That he the said Eloze Abramye Israel
shall be hanged by the neck until he be dead—